8/04

305.23

||||||| P9-DBL-340

WM ADAMS BACHELDER LIBRARY
POB 128 EAST ANDOVER NH 03231

DISCARDED BY WM. BACHELDER
LIBRARY

Mean Chicks, Cliques, and Dirty Tricks

305.2
Karres, Erika V. Shearin
Mean chicks, cliques, and dirty
tricks

NOV 1 2 2004

FEB 4

DISCARDED BY WM. BACHELDER
LIBRARY

Mean Chicks, Cliques, and Dirty Tricks

A Real Girl's Guide to Getting Through the Day with Smarts and Style

Erika V. Shearin Karres, Ed.D.

A

Adams Media
Avon, Massachusetts

Copyright ©2004, Erika V. Shearin Karres, Ed.D. All rights reserved.
This book, or parts thereof, may not be reproduced in any form
without permission from the publisher; exceptions are made
for brief excerpts used in published reviews.

Published by
Adams Media, an F+W Publications Company
57 Littlefield Street, Avon MA 02322. U.S.A.
www.adamsmedia.com

ISBN: 1-58062-933-4

Printed in the United States of America.

J   I   H   G   F   E   D   C   B   A

Library of Congress Cataloging-in-Publication Data
Karres, Erika V. Shearin.
Mean chicks, cliques, and dirty tricks / by Erika V. Shearin Karres.
p.   cm.
Summary: A guide for coping with girls who are mean to other girls,
using the words of teenagers to explore how the meanness can get
started, forms it may take, and what can be done to stop it.
ISBN 1-58062-933-4
1. Teenage girls—Juvenile literature. 2. Teenage
girls—Psychology—Juvenile literature. 3. Interpersonal conflict in
adolescence—Juvenile literature. [1. Teenage girls. 2. Interpersonal
relations. 3. Conflict management.] I. Title.
HQ798.K35 2004
305.235'2—dc22
2003012548

This publication is designed to provide accurate and authoritative information with regard to the subject matter covered. It is sold with the understanding that the publisher is not engaged in rendering legal, accounting, or other professional advice. If legal advice or other expert assistance is required, the services of a competent professional person should be sought.
—From a *Declaration of Principles* jointly adopted by a Committee of the American Bar Association and a Committee of Publishers and Associations

Many of the designations used by manufacturers and sellers to distinguish their products are claimed as trademarks. Where those designations appear in this book and Adams Media was aware of a trademark claim, the designations have been printed with initial capital letters.

This book is available at quantity discounts for bulk purchases.
For information, call 1-800-872-5627.

Contents

Dedication

This book is for Elizabeth S. Hounshell and Dr. Mary D. Shearin, my daughters, and for Andrew M. Karres, my husband, with all my love and thanks.

Also for June Clark, my cutting-edge literary agent.

And for Rebecca Carpenter for Internet research.

And for Danielle Chiotti and Kate Epstein, my editors at Adams Media. They did a superb job condensing my extensive research down to its core and made it accessible to girls ages ten and up. As a result, many major obstacles that used to keep girls from reaching their full potential can now be recognized, removed, and rooted out. Forever.

On behalf of girls now and in the future: Thank you, Danielle and Kate! You're our heroines.

Acknowledgments

A very special thanks to all the girls who participated in my research and to my thoughtful teen readers and experts. And to Jim Jackson, a master teacher who has instructed and inspired tens of thousands of students.

And to Bettina Grahek. What a powerful educator and school leader she is!

Introduction

First Words

Don't Let Anyone Get in Your Way!

Please don't let anyone get in your way! You're a girl *now* during the best time in the history of the world to be one. What does this mean? What an incredible life you have ahead of you. You have so many choices, so many opportunities, so many resources. Things your mom, grandmother, and perhaps even your older sister could only dream of are right at your fingertips. And now that you're a teenager, you're at the beginning of these most exciting times.

Yes, it's all starting to happen—the thrilling times you were looking forward to—like having a *bunch* more freedom, independence, and a later curfew. You may be looking forward to moving on to middle or high school and all the cool extracurricular activities you love, like soccer, drama, and the school dances—even dating and maybe a steady boyfriend.

Sure, you're coming more and more into your own by testing the waters of the hottest fashions and styles, by defining your personal tastes, and finding what you like and what you loathe. But most of all, right now is when you start standing on your own two feet and relating to your friends in a closer way. Now the camaraderie of other girls really rules, and all of you can have tons of fun.

The Expert

Things are way different from when I grew up. I had a harsh childhood in post–World War II Germany. My mother died when I was six, my stepmother had lots of nervous breakdowns, I had ten brothers and sisters, and we never had any money. When I was twelve years old, I didn't even have enough money for some "feminine hygiene products" and had to use wads of scratchy toilet paper!

But I always had one thing—the determination to make sure other girls didn't have it as rough as I did, that they wouldn't have anything or *anyone get in their way!* That's why I became a teacher and later, what I am now—Dr. Erika, an advice giver who listens to and helps girls in particular.

In pursuit of this dream, I got the necessary education and job experience. Later, my own daughters grew up to become accomplished and productive adults. So after a horrible start, my life turned out great. My happy life in America made up for all those miserable years when I was just trying to survive. And what a joy it is, in return, to be able to pay back this great country by my work as an author and girl guru.

1,000 Teen Girls

While writing this book, I polled more than 1,000 teen girls who attend various middle and high schools, from small to large, and asked them (or had their teachers ask them) the following: "What, in your opinion, is a major problem for girls today?"

The girls blurted out, "Other girls! *They get in our way* because they're so mean." Their teachers agreed, saying, "That's right. We see signs of girls' acting aggressively on a daily basis."

So I went back to the girls and asked, "Have you ever been a victim of girls being mean or been witness to it?" And without exception they all nodded, "Yes!" And some of the girls felt so strongly about the topic that they started peppering me with e-mails, which I call "fe-mails."

 I think every girl has been hurt in some way or made fun of by another girl or a group of girls once in their life. ⁓ Brianne, 15

A Veil of Silence

But when I asked the girls to give me some details on the behavior of their peers, silence settled over them like a thick veil. Their only response was to roll their eyes.

 To ask a girl if she's ever been treated mean by another girl or girls is to ask if she's ever been around her peers. ∼Dory, 16

Whoa! It turned out that the subject of mean girls was actually taboo! And the teachers' responses? These were even worse; they *really* clammed up. Yet, like the girls, they admitted that the treatment among girls is a huge problem in their schools.

 I don't know any girls that don't hurt other girls in some ways. Why? Because life is tough for girls. It treats us like a baby does a diaper. ∼Angela, 14

Could it be that the teachers were afraid to have one more job on their plates? Or were they afraid they'd have to change their teaching methods?

Heroines

Whatever the teachers' reasons, a few girls were heroines by opening up to me. Personal stories poured in when I told them that I did not want to know:

- ★ Their names.
- ★ The names of their schools.
- ★ Their teachers' names.
- ★ The names of their towns, cities, or states.
- ★ Anything that could identify them, their parents and families, or their backgrounds in any way.

I began receiving buckets of mail, oh, how furiously they wrote.

 Have you ever made fun of another girl? If your answer is no, more than likely you're lying. If your answer is yes, you're not totally a bad person. You're just telling it like it is. ～Annie, 16

Soon, I had stacks of letters about the realities of girls hurting other girls, and how painful it is to be the butt of their cruel jokes or to be picked on for their looks.

 I've been picked on about my hair all my life because I have curly and bushy hair. My best friends call my hair "nappy roots" and laugh. ～Natasha, 17

It's tough to be laughed at. Or pinched or kicked, for that matter! Having rumors spread about you is certainly no fun. And while I could easily sense the pain of the victims, the victimizers clearly needed help, too, and ASAP!

So, now help is here! You are reading this book. Because you picked it up, you show that you care and want to make the girl world a better place.

 Making fun of other girls is not my thing. I know that they have feelings just like myself. ～Ellie, 15

So you're a heroine, too, because you want to do what you can to help. Only, there's one problem: How can you spot the mean girl types? And how can you get a handle on them now and in the years to come? And, more importantly, how can you help them?

Most of all, how can you be sure *not to let anyone get in your way*? Read on.

Part I

Random Acts of Unkindness

F ace it. Even if you haven't met any mean girls in person yet, they exist in every school, and that's a fact. So what can you do, should they target *you*? A whole lot!

First, you can use your potential and your power to learn all about them: about the way they act and what makes them tick. Then you can learn how to disarm and defuse them, to stop them in their tracks! At the very least, you can learn to refuse being overly irritated by them. You see, you really are special. You're the new girl, the *now* girl, the one who will run the show shortly if she isn't already. There's no other girl in the world with your smarts, looks, and heart.

You're the leader of the future and these are *your* years! So don't let anything or anyone stop you on your quest to be the best.

The truth is, some girls can do some way mean things. They can be flat-out unkind, openly ignoring other girls, picking on them, or actually hurting them physically. If you haven't seen them, you no doubt will shortly. But don't worry—you have the power to get on top of this situation and benefit from it.

I believe that there's a purpose or a lesson to be learned in every event that occurs in someone's life. You reap what you sow. Next time you decide to diss someone always remember, what goes around comes around.
~Jeni, 16

So, by the end of this book, you'll be able to spot whatever not-nice girl acts are out there, in all their many nasty, sneaky, or hidden ways. Fact is, some mean girl behavior isn't immediately obvious. It can be covered up with a syrupy smile or disguised in some other way. Hey, some mean chicks might even look attractive when observed from a distance.

But they're not! Like, for instance, take a look at "The Snob."

A word of caution: No matter what people call the mean girls at your school—snobs, gossips, traitors, and so forth—behind their backs, let's get one thing absolutely straight first: When we discuss the kinds of mean girl behaviors that exist today, we are going to use these same terms, but only to save time. That is, rather than to say a girl has tendencies to act like a snob most of the time, we're just going to generalize and call her a "Snob," and so on. But under no circumstances does that mean she will *always* be a snob, or that we should forever condemn or demonize her. Anyway, it's not the girl we're criticizing; it's only her way of acting or treating other girls. So, we might not like her actions or the way she expresses herself, but it never means we don't like the girl. Underneath, she has what all girls have—tons of potential and a terrific future ahead.

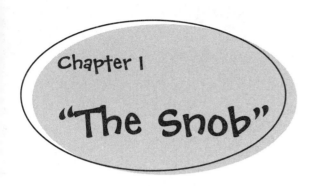

Chapter 1

"The Snob"

Words to Live By: No one can make you feel inferior without your consent. ~Eleanor Roosevelt

What Makes a Girl a Snob?

You see her cruising with her gal pals in her brand-new convertible, shopping at the most expensive stores, and getting away with murder at school. The slightest glance toward her in the halls can either make your day or ruin it, depending on her mood. Her hair is always perfect; her clothes just right. She dates the cutest guys and has all of the teachers wrapped around her finger. She has the best parties and the coolest friends. You've just encountered . . . "the Snob."

Dear Dr. Erika:

There's this girl in my class who thinks whenever she opens her big mouth everybody better shut up and listen. And at lunch she sits at the best table in the cafeteria, and woe! if you park there. She pitches a fit. She actually gets her way in everything. Even the teachers are scared of her and treat her different from the rest of us.

~Reina, 14

Dear Dr. Erika:

I dread my second period class. There's this girl who, like, brags about everything. When she makes a good grade, she acts like she's the smartest. When she has a birthday party, she goes, like, "There's never been another party like mine." When she blabs about her family, they're like sooo rich! And she cuts people and makes me feel like I'm dirt.

~Erica, 15

Sounds as if both Reina and Erica are dealing with the Snob, sometimes called "a spoiled brat," other times "the Brag" or "Name-Dropper."

FYI

No matter what type of show she may put on at school or with her friends, try to remember that the Snob is just a girl with problems, worries, hopes, and fears. Just like you! Sure, the Snob's issues may be a little different from yours. Most likely, for all of her cool clothes and popularity, deep down, she feels unhappy. She feels as if there's a big hole in her—like she's always trying to fill a void within herself. Maybe she was spoiled as a child and everything was done for her. Or maybe her parents got divorced and she was ignored and now wants what she didn't get before—namely, attention. But the most likely scenario is that the Snob never got the one thing all little girls everywhere want—and that's a steady stream of love and attention from her mom or dad. What this girl *did* get instead is material things—and plenty of them. Whoever raised the Snob had no time for her and tried to make up for it with oodles of doodads. So now the Snob covers up her hollow part inside by overemphasizing stuff.

She gets her kicks out of shopping and mall crawling. What she adores are fancy designer shoes, Louis Vuitton pocketbooks, serious jewelry. Also she sees people as things—as expensive, classy items to enrich herself with. In the process, she doesn't necessarily mean to be rude, but comes across as arrogant and selfish. She has to have her way all the time and acts like a baby crying, "Me, me, me!" because that's all she knows. Her value system and her self-esteem are based on what valuables she has. So she carries on like a mini queen, like the princess bee in the family. In school she's often the most popular girl in her grade even though—behind her back—many students call her a spoiled brat.

A close cousin to the Snob is the Name-Dropper. That's a girl who might not have been showered with tons of toys, but her family knows famous folks. Or maybe she used to go to kindergarten with a relative of President John F. Kennedy, or the child of a former neighbor of President George W. Bush. So instead of getting her self-esteem from *stuff*, which the Snob, "Brat," and "Brag" do, the Name-Dropper gets hers from dropping famous names. Oh, how she loves to mention the most popular guy in the senior class, the top athlete, or the "player" who's getting all the scholarship offers. She seems to know them all or at least the inside scoop about them.

Instead of focusing on what they can do to better themselves, the Snob and her cousins focus on what they have—the latest Gucci bags, Dior dresses, or Manolo Blahnik boots—and measure what others have (or don't have) against their own possessions.

But don't be fooled by her exterior—it's very possible that stripped of her fancy clothes or friends, the Snob has the same insecurities as everyone else. Even though she's sporting the latest Kate Spade bag or the hottest new haircut as she prances down the halls with her entourage, maybe she's worried about the fight she overheard her parents having the night before or the history quiz in third period.

 If you go around judging other girls as beneath you all the time, you can't concentrate on what's most important—getting to be your personal best. ⌒ Chaka, 15

But rather than fess up and confide in a good friend, the Snob wants other girls to feel miserable, too. This stems from her inability to face up to the fact that all isn't hunky-dory in her life. So she dishes out plenty of needlelike remarks in an attempt to make herself feel better.

 If you're making yourself feel better by ignoring other girls on purpose, you obviously have not been feeling great. ⌒ Annyce, 17

How true. The Snob and her close cousins never seem to feel that great. Why else would they act the way they do?

Isn't it a shame that some girls feel so low they have to raise themselves up by making other girls feel low? ～Tierra, 18

The fact is, no girl ever feels really good inside when she's putting other girls down. Sure, she may get a rush of so-called superiority but it's only temporary.

What you have got to do is look at yourself first and see what's wrong with you before you criticize other girls and look down on them. ～Flora, 15

Having trouble believing that the Snob could ever have problems? Let's take a look at Tierney.

Universal High School

Tierney attends Universal High School, but not the way most girls do, either riding the bus, being dropped off by a parent, or riding with an older sibling. Uh-uh, not Tierney. Most every school day morning, she zooms into the parking lot in her brand-new Beemer just before the tardy bell. She hops out of the car with her best girl pals in tow, and then, with her shiny mane swinging, she dashes into school, where she deliberately slows down to a snail's pace, all the time giggling and making plans for lunch.

No need to hurry. She knows if she slides into her seat by the last ring of the late bell, she won't be marked as tardy. And even if she's not on time, no teacher would dare mark her down. Tierney has a way of coming up with more believable excuses than you can imagine. And she delivers each one with such fake sincerity that you think, "Hmm, maybe it's true?" Plus, it's who her parents are—Tierney's dad is a big shot, and so is her mom.

And should someone sit in Tierney's preferred seat, in the middle of the room where she's surrounded by all her friends, she just stands by that desk, rolls her eyes, and sighs—until the unsuspecting student hops up in embarrassment and moves to a corner of the room.

When the teacher assigns group work and puts a girl that Tierney doesn't associate with into her group, Tierney rolls her eyes some more (Nerd Alert!) until that girl hurriedly asks to trade places with one of Tierney's friends. Should the teacher ever protest, that "nobody" girl gets frozen out during group work. No one will talk to her. Or maybe "Tierney & Co." will say something nasty to the "nerd" girl, make her do all the hard or dirty work on the group project, and pronto! You know, take the notes, do the footnotes, cover the longest and most boring chapters, that type of thing . . . whatever Tierney and her gal pals don't want to do. In the meantime, they talk about what dresses they're going to wear to the prom, pulling out *Vogue* and *Cosmo* while with an eager smile the "nerd" hops to it, so pleased to be allowed to do the grunt work.

When classes are over for the day, there's cheerleading practice, and Tierney and her friends report to the gym, but again in no hurry. Although most of her many friends are not on the squad, Tierney is, and she knows that practice won't start until she shows up. That's just the way it's always been. After practice, the girls all pile into her Beemer and grab a latte with skim milk at the Dairy Bar. Tierney drops her friends off at home one by one and then heads home herself.

As she pulls into the driveway, she can tell no one is home by the absence of cars. Wow, for once she's all alone. Her girl buds will come over later, naturally, like they do every day. But for the moment the house is empty, which is a weird feeling. She almost hates to go inside, but she does.

Tierney kicks the front door shut, drops her books on a table, and hurries upstairs. She flops onto her bed for a moment, thinking, "What do I do now?" She strides into her walk-in closet, which is crammed with the hottest clothes. Most everything has been worn only once, if even. In one corner sits a pile of shopping bags from brand-name stores that she hasn't unpacked yet. Great—something to do!

As she hangs up the new jeans and sweaters, she runs her hands over them, hoping to feel better. For a moment she remembers how life used to be before her parents got divorced. They had time for her then. Mom wasn't gone all the time; and Dad used to call her "his girl" and they would do stuff together. Now she sees him maybe twice a month. But, hey, he just gave her another credit card, with no limit—so that's something, right?

Tierney stops unpacking stuff and calls her best friends. "Before pizza here, why don't we all meet at the Nordstrom make-up counter?" And tomorrow Tierney will come to school in yet another great outfit, her friends surrounding her as they talk about what happened after they ate the pizza, giving other girls a "you don't count" stare.

 But isn't the point of being popular to have friends? So why would you want to make enemies by acting like you're <u>too good</u> for other girls? It's senseless. ∼ Marie, 15

What you need to keep in mind is that underneath the Snob (or Snobs) is a girl who may not be so different from you—she may be a real nice girl just trying to emerge. Yet meanwhile you still have to suffer from her actions. Or do you?

Take this quiz to find out if you can hold your own against the Snob.

<FAST QUIZ>

Snob Susceptibility—How Vulnerable Are You?

1. The Snob in your classes or among your group of friends has to have her way all the time. In order to deal with her, you:

   a. Stay as invisible as possible—it's better than getting on her bad side.

b. Go along with her wishes, hoping she'll invite you to hang out with her sometime.

c. Speak out against her whenever you get the chance—you're not going to let her push you around!

d. Treat her the same as you would treat anyone else—she's no more special than the rest of your classmates.

2. You're in study hall reading a magazine when the Snob sashays over to you, asking in a sugary voice if she can borrow your algebra homework—she forgot hers at home. You:

a. Make up an excuse to avoid helping her out—better to avoid her than to rock the boat.

b. Jump at the chance to do something for her—you never know where it will get you.

c. Give her your sweetest smile and give her your algebra homework—from last week!

d. Tell her you don't let anyone copy your homework—but offer your help after school if she's having trouble.

3. You've been really pumped about auditioning for the lead in the school play. When you walk into the auditorium on the day of the tryouts, you realize the Snob is auditioning as well. You:

a. Sneak out of the auditorium as quietly as possible before anyone sees you—why bother? She always gets the lead anyway.

b. Rush up to her and tell her how perfect she is for the part. You're probably better off in the chorus, anyway.

c. March up to her and let her know she's got no claim on the part—and tell her she's tone deaf!

d. Get on stage and sing your heart out—better to give it your best than not to try at all.

4. You've been eyeing the most perfect pair of shoes for months and you finally have the money to buy them. You show up at school dressed to kill and ready to show off your shoes when you spot the Snob swishing down the hall in the very same shoes! You:

a. Haul your butt to the nearest bathroom, lock yourself in a stall, and don't come out until your girlfriends have scored you another pair of shoes—back to the drawing board!

b. Make sure you "just happen" to walk by her locker while she's standing there so she'll "notice" that you have the same shoes. Compliment her on her taste and apologize for having the same pair—they look better on her anyway.

c. Say "Oh, look, we have the same shoes! How cute! Wow, I never realized that your feet were SOOO BIG! It must be really hard for you to find your size!"

d. Don't make a big deal of it—you know you look great. With so many girls in one place, you're bound to have this dilemma once in a while.

Now it's time to find out how you did. Total up your answers. How many A's, B's, C's, or D's do you have? For

3 or 4 A's
check out Answer 1.

3 or 4 C's
check out Answer 3.

3 or 4 B's
check out Answer 2.

3 or 4 D's
check out Answer 4.

But if you have a mixture of A's, B's, C's, and D's, look at all the answers. Obviously, there's a little bit of everything in you, which is great. Now, can you work on having a little less of the Answer 1 attitude and a little more of the Answer 4 attitude?

Answers

1. Invisible Girl

Okay, so we all know that the Snob can be intimidating, even on her best days, but that's no reason to deny yourself happiness. You're allowing the Snob to have too much power over you and your decisions. Remember, seen in the light of day, even a firefly is just an ordinary insect. You have a right to be whoever you want to be. This is your time to shine—don't let the actions of others affect your potential.

2. Kiss Up

Whoa, girl! You've got to give yourself a bit of a reality check! So are sooo at the mercy of the Snob! You've got to quit it, from this moment on. You can't live your whole life trying to please someone else, or soon you'll find you have nothing left that pleases *you*. You don't have to dance to her tune or give in to her whims anymore. Do you think your popularity will suffer if you stand up for what you want to do? When you let the Snob get away with her behavior, you're an enabler. Don't be one. Take a stand; be yourself. You may be amazed at what happens.

3. Sassy Cathy

Good for you! You make sure to speak your mind and not to let the Snob take advantage of you. However, winning through disrespect to someone else may not be your best bet. So, you stand up to her, but at what cost? You've got a life and lots of stuff to do—why add to your busy schedule by starting a war with the Snob? Keep up your strong attitude, but be ready to face the consequences of your not-so-nice actions!

4. Amazing Attitude

You go, girl! Pat yourself on the back—you've got it all together. You're an independent-minded girl who can recognize the Snob from a mile away and that's that. No way you'll ever let her get you down. You know your limits, and you handle yourself like a pro—calm, cool, and collected, that's your motto!

But no matter how you handle the Snob/Brat in your pack, know there's always at least one in any bunch of girls.

Snob Smarts: What Should You Know about the Snob?

- ★ Understand that the Snob has a problem that has nothing to do with you. Deep inside, she is insecure. She wants to cover up her insecurity and make herself feel better at your expense.
- ★ While it's so common for girls to feel this way, try not to be fooled. Just know that the problem belongs to the Snob, not to you. Condemn her *behavior*, not her.

 I always felt I was not good enough for any of them. That's the way the other girls were treating me, but that was wrong. ～Mandee, 15

Correct, so next time you feel less than great in the face of the Snob, just think about the fact that maybe she isn't feeling so terrific on the inside. But you are and you have a plan. Move ahead.

- ★ Also, if you feel like it, try to become the Snob's friend. She might really need one *real* friend. So make a list of what is positive about her and see where you go from there. You might be amazed at how extending the hand of friendship can turn another person around.

However, until you have decided how you feel about the Snob, what you need is a quick solution right now.

Rapid Response: What You Should Do about the Snob

There are number of things you can do to disarm the Snob and take away some of her power over you. Here are three to consider:

1. Be tough as you go through your school day. Draw on your inner strength and know you're as good as everybody else. So there's no need to avoid the Snob—*ever*—unless it's because you don't have time for her foolish games.

2. Be as helpful as you can, if the Snob wants your help. However, be friendly but firm. Don't turn her down just because she's the Snob! Just make sure she's not taking advantage of your nice-girl nature.

3. Be prepared. Have a few kind but knockout, disarming stares or statements ready for whatever "superior" lines the Snob might lob your way. Practice these statements: "I'm glad you're doing so well" (when the Snob brags about her fabulous possessions). Or, "Sorry you're having a bad day" (when the Snob disses you or your friends by flouncing away from you, with her nose held high). Or, "The main thing is, you like them" (when the Snob drops the names of her friends, the Hollywood superstars). Meanwhile, practice being modest and friendly to everyone. We teach best by example.

First Person: What I Went Through—A Real Life Story

When I was in the eighth grade, we moved to another state and I had to go to school with a bunch of girls who were from a real nice neighborhood. And they never let me forget it. There was one girl in particular. She would gush about her perfect pool parties constantly and the cabana they had in her yard that was way bigger than a house! And how much fun they had cooking out on their humongous patio. This kind of talk went on year round.

Needless to say, all the other girls got invited but not me. Never me, uh-uh. This went on for two years. Then my dad got a big promotion and we bought a place at the lake. Dad said I could invite anybody I wanted anytime, but I waited for the right moment. Finally, when we were juniors, I volunteered to head up the prom committee, which was a big deal. We had to make the most important decisions about the theme, the color scheme, the music, the food, the caterer. We had to pick out the photographers, order the invitations, get stuff mailed and approved, come up with the rules—I mean we had the power to decide every sweet detail that mattered. Wow. There were twelve of us, and I made sure I asked them all to the lake for an epic planning session, plus the advisors too. But I made doubly sure the invitation to Ms. Cabana got "lost."

~*Shoshana, 17*

First Rate: Grade the Girls

C- Good for you, Shoshana, for taking the initiative to do something cool for yourself and your school. You stood tall in the face of the Snob and made smart decisions for yourself. But then when the tide had turned and you were in a position to show how much of a leader you had become, you wimped out at a critical moment. You had such a great chance to set the record straight! You should have taken this opportunity to clear the air: to invite Ms. Cabana, but with a note attached, saying something like: *For two years you have not invited me to any of your pool parties, but that was your choice. My choice is to have you come to our lake house so we all can work on the prom preps together. You may feel awkward about accepting my invitation, but do try to come. . . .*

Something like that would have taught her a lesson. More importantly, it would have helped you grow. Revenge is a nasty motive—it's sneaky and it can be cruel. By mimicking Ms. Cabana's snotty actions, you enable her to keep acting like a snot. You'd better watch yourself in the future or you could end up turning into a Ms. Cabana yourself.

Dear Diary

Now that you've nailed down your snob susceptibility, you probably have a pretty clear picture of where you stand. In the presence of the Snob, do you turn into a meek lamb? Or do you tell her what the *real* score is? No matter what your answer, chances are that there has been a time when someone said something totally rude to you or about you—as if you didn't count!—and that hurt your feelings. If that ever happened, it's time to get it off your chest.

Get out an old notebook; you know, the one that's almost empty from your least favorite class. Then, recycle that ratty-looking leftover notebook as your personal journal. Whenever you read something in this book that sparks an idea or thought, jot it down. You may be surprised at how much better it makes you feel and how much you can learn about yourself! Throughout this book, there will be several journal exercises for you. Have fun with them, and don't be afraid to express your feelings. Here's a little exercise to start you out:

Are you totally bothered by the Snob in your class or your group of friends? Are there things she says or does that make you feel bad about yourself? We've all felt bad about ourselves at one time or another. It's just an unpleasant fact of life that we have to deal with—kind of like having a bad hair day or a pop history quiz. Now, make a list of five things that make you feel bad about yourself in the face of the Snob. They can be anything at all, be it something she said to you or thoughts or feelings you have—don't hold back. After you've made your list, jot down a few sentences (or pages if you wish) that explain how these things make you feel. It's okay to get mad or sad or whatever—this is your personal journal.

Now, let's take those negative feelings and turn them around! Next to each of the negative items, write five things that you love about yourself. Jot down a few sentences (or pages) about the things that make you feel good about yourself. It's okay to celebrate yourself every once in a while. In fact, it's a great reminder of the good things in your life.

Finally, examine your lists closely and compare them. The next time you're around the Snob or faced with any situation that makes you feel bad, think of the good things from your list and remind yourself that you and only you have the power to create your own happiness. Congratulations! You've just made an attitude adjustment.

 Acting like you're so superior is a sure sign of ignorance to me. I hope girls all over the world are smart enough to just ignore that ignorance and rise above it.
~ Raine, 14

Fab Fixes for Whatever Attitude Ails You

What's one of the best things about being a girl? Our ability to accessorize! Sure, one day you're into retro garb, the next into celeb styles, the third into grungy dungarees. Whatever inspires you, right?

Well, it's the same with attitudes. Many days you have a great attitude, even the best, don't you? But there are times when you feel like being totally different, like being a real pain in the a _ _ , for example. You've got these mood swings that can send you from Suzy Sunshine to Courtney Love in thirty seconds flat. So who knows—you might slam doors, shrug, and not respond when your mom asks you something. You may clomp around the house, mumble and mutter under your breath, or maybe you act like a total snob. Suddenly, you're *so superior* to your friends or siblings.

This never lasts long, but it does happen. So what to do when you have a case of bad attitude, in other words, when you feel like being a snob and have a real "Brattitude"?

Rx—Battling Brattitude

Check out some of these tips to improve your 'tude, no matter what kind of day you're having. Do 3x a day:

1. Look in the mirror and laugh at yourself. Do you really like that snobby, pouty, or brattish expression on your face? You know that the way we frown gets etched into our faces, don't

you? Wouldn't you rather have laugh lines than bitter, sour-lemon ones as you get older?

2. Say you're sorry to all those people you were snobby or snooty to. Start today.

3. Do something nice for somebody else. This is a sure fix to getting your attitude back on track. Write a letter to a friend, clean the kitchen for your mom, take your little brother to see the latest Disney cartoon. Okay, so it might not be as cool as the newest J-Lo flick, but it's sure to be a good time.

It's amazing how making someone else smile can improve your disposition. Chances are, you'll end up smiling yourself and losing that brattitude. Remember, it's okay to have a bad day now and then, but acting like a clone of the Snob or allowing her behavior to influence your attitude is definitely *not* cool. By letting yourself shine, you'll encourage others to shine, too!

The Bottom Line

You know, just because some girls in school shine and attract lots of attention and even get special privileges from some of their teachers, they might be nothing but a firefly or lightning bug. What does that mean? Well, seen in twilight, a firefly may appear to shine brightly. However, seen in bright daylight, that firefly is nothing more than a little insect—a little insect that's got everyone fooled but you.

So, try not to be taken in by the surface appearance of any girl in your school. Instead, try to look beneath the outer appearance. You will examine what's going on with girls like Tierney. You could actually just close your eyes to the way the Tierneys among us act and wait until their popularity wanes, which it will sooner or later (trust me!) or until someone even more popular comes along and disses them.

But by checking in with yourself and with the girl teen scene at your school, you will be able to affirm what's good, abolish what's bad, and improve things overall. So know that you can do it: deal with the Snob or her cousins at your school or in your group of friends. Remember that she's someone who may be in pain and that her attitude and actions *only* affect you if you let them. So don't worry about her. Instead, focus on the incredible choices you have around you now and those that are waiting for you in the future.

Should you ever find any snob/brat feelings in yourself, suppress them or swat them away like a gnat. Scram, they're gone! Feeling superior to other girls because you have a bigger allowance or live in a nicer home or because your 'rents make way more money is very uncool.

Remember, you're never alone. You have your friends. And now, you have this book and your journal to help you through those tough moments. Think of them like you think of your favorite pair of sweatpants or blue jeans—so comfy and familiar— knowing they'll always be there when you need them. Simply think of dealing with a snob or spoiled brat as a bump in the road—something that's got to be watched out for, stepped over, then put behind you just like *that* . . . with the snap of your fingers.

 No matter what you do, some girls will always think you're less than they are and not worth anything. What that really means is that they are immature and have a long way to go. ～ Kristi, 17

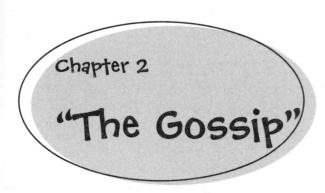

Chapter 2

"The Gossip"

Words to Live By: Worry less about what other people think about you, and more about what you think about them. —Fay Weldon

What Makes a Girl a Gossip?

She's always bustling about the hallways with the latest buzz—who's dating who, who got suspended, whatever! She's super-sweet to your face when she wants the scoop, but once she gets it—watch out! This girl can be a handful. She spied on a note you wrote in algebra class and now it's all over the school. She saw you talking to your best friend's boyfriend and now everyone thinks you're a man-stealer! She's sweet . . . she's conversational . . . and she's sassy. You've just encountered . . . "the Gossip."

> Dear Dr. Erika:
>
> Being two-faced—that's what I hate more than anything. But there's this girl on my bus who acts so goody-goody. She starts talking to me and saying nice things. Then I hear from another friend what she says about me behind my back and the way she, like, runs me in the ground and calls me names and stuff. And before I know it, the fact that I stumbled gets twisted into me being "drunk." By lunch everybody is talking about it. That afternoon, girls I don't even know whisper mean things about me.
>
> But whenever I confront the girl who started the rumor, she denies everything and acts so innocent, it kills me.
>
> ~Dee Dee, 15

Dear Dr. Erika:

I am so upset I don't know what to do. For years and years I was kinda big. I mean besides having these large bones that run in my family. So what I did was ask the guidance department at my school to help me. They sent me to the cafeteria manager. She's a cool lady who gave me a bunch of books. Pamphlets actually. But anyway, I read them from cover to cover. Then spring break came and I thought: Aah! What a perfect time. So while my friends went off to the beach I said I wasn't feeling well and stayed home and started fixing myself some low-cal stuff to eat. You know, toasted bagel with low-fat cream cheese for breakfast, salad for lunch, and tuna and veggies for dinner. Stuff like that. And for sure, no more junk food. I dropped a couple of pounds during the first two weeks and ever since I've been losing more weight. Nothing drastic but slow and steady just like those books tell you to. And now everyone at school's saying I have anorexia! Even though I owned up about the dieting, now my "best" friend is spreading rumors about what I eat or not.

~Snow, 14

FYI

"The Gossip," and her cousin, "the Backstabber," seem to think they're hip when in fact they're just shooting from the lip. Gossips are busybodies carrying around something they heard like a plate of goodies they're offering to guests at a reception. The Gossip is always dishing the latest scoop, and oh, does she have lots to talk about. Most of what she has to say is 99 percent negative and is never about her. Instead, the Gossip picks up a tiny tasty tidbit of news and then she's off, flitting from friend to friend like a busy bee going from flower to flower, embellishing hugely on whatever she's heard. The bummer about the Gossip is that she *could* be a really good friend—she's tons of fun to talk to and she's a great communicator. But beware of the charms of the Gossip. Though it may seem like she's listening to your latest boy troubles with a sympathetic ear, when you share with the Gossip, you may find that your problems have been spread through the entire school before lunch. Instead of using her talents for a good cause, like writing for the school newspaper, she uses her skills for no good at all.

You see, the problem with the Gossip is that she desperately wants to be admired and to feel like she's on top while you're not. Gossiping is the only way she knows to do that.

 How do you feel when someone gossips about you? Do you feel down? Low? Does it "mess" with your self-esteem? Sure it does. ～Brynne, 13

The Gossip is really self-aggrandizing and doesn't care whom she hurts. She's trying to make herself ever-so-scintillating by being in the know and spreading juicy jabber around the school. She's trying to build herself up with importance while bringing other girls down.

Imagine how much the Gossip could accomplish by climbing a ladder of real achievements rather than stepping on the backs of some girls who either don't know they're being gossiped about or are too polite or shy to speak up.

 To be gossiped about is a gut-wrenching feeling. That's why I love to do it—my amusement at some other girl's expense. The feeling is all-mighty. But afterward I sometimes feel bad. ～Lindsey, 17

So while the Gossip can be dangerous, don't write her off just yet. Gossiping, as I'm sure you know, is very fun.

 You feel powerful and popular by amusing other girls with your stories, well, <u>lies</u>, about other girls. However it's way different when the joke is on you. ～Abby, 17

Oftentimes the Gossip is just a teenager who needs an outlet for her talents so she won't turn on innocent classmates. She's really a people person—perhaps just a little misguided.

Maybe she only wanted dirt on you up until now because she hasn't had any other alternative. Just give her something to dish about that's not bad. Let her be the girl who reads the daily school announcements over the intercom! Or perhaps investigative journalism might be her thing—with her nose for news, she could probably win a Pulitzer!

"The Backstabber"

A close cousin of the Gossip is the Backstabber. Whereas the gossip is more of a town crier but in a secretive way, the Backstabber has two personalities: two sides like a double-sided mirror. On side A, she ingratiates herself to you, acting nice and sweet until you confide in her. Then she takes that bit of info that you told her confidentially, embellishes it, and passes it on to anyone willing to listen.

On side B, she joins the crowd of listeners and actually makes fun of the exact same girl she was formerly so nice to. So she betrays your trust, plus often ends up being one of the biggest fun-makers herself. Maybe she thinks whatever she's doing is just good-natured kidding about a girl who's not present, but it goes far beyond it.

 Backstabbing is about the worst you can do. It makes the girl who's stabbed in the back feel like she can't ever trust anybody again. It could affect her for her whole life! ⁓ Suzanne, 15

Universal High School

With her glistening, black hair short and straight, her beautiful bright, dark-brown eyes, and her ever-ready smile, Nikki is everywhere at Universal High. One moment she's in the office, handing in a computer attendance sheet the student assistant forgot to pick up from Nikki's homeroom teacher. The next moment she's in the guidance department talking to the secretary about a college in California she heard about: Do you have a catalog from Berkeley?

The secretary smiles back: No, not at the moment, but I can request one.

Would you please? Nikki asks. It's urgent!

Just last night Nikki examined herself critically again, so pleased with the way she looks. But why can't she grow?

At five foot six, she's way too short to become a model, which is what she wants in a most major way. Correction: It's what she wanted, but no more. Since it doesn't seem like she's ever going to be over six feet tall, she's now thinking of going into business and open up a modeling school. Does the University of Berkeley even have a business program for this, she thinks.

After leaving the guidance department, Nikki dashes to the cultural arts wing. The dance teacher told Nikki she would teach her how to walk properly. Of course, by then the bell has rung, but Nikki still has that pass from her homeroom teacher, so she's okay. "The office was, like, sooo busy" will be her excuse, and Nikki rehearses it to herself as she stops in the rest room. Here, she uses the fingers of one hand to count up all the juicy tidbits she overheard this morning. There was that thing about the chairman of the English department going home with the flu, the dish on the fight in the hall just before homeroom, and the class ring order date being set for next week. Now for the real inside scoop. The captain of the football team was being fussed out in the principal's office, and that tall new girl was in the hall without a pass again! Even better, the candidate for homecoming queen was being checked up on by her own mom. Nikki overheard the incoming phone call: "Just checking that my daughter made it to first period today, blah-blah-blah . . ."

But Nikki knows that she didn't. She saw Little Miss Homecoming with her own eyes totally skipping first period and reading *Jane* in the library! Oh, so much to tell her friends, so much to fill everybody in on . . .

For a moment Nikki pauses and smiles to herself. She's going over all the bits of gossip she's picked up so far and will gladly spread, but why? Because it makes her so pow-erful and so charming, admired—and so much in charge. Girls and guys, no matter what their cliques, want to talk to *her* to get the scoop. She loves being the center of attention, smiling for the crowd, feeling all of those eyes on her. Unlike what happens to her at home, where there is an atmosphere of rush, rush, rush, and gloom and doom. Her parents are hard workers, but recently their store rent was increased, so they had to move their business home into their living room. Now both Mom and Dad work furiously, but the more they work, the less they seem to make. The economy's just not too hot right now. What if things get worse and worse? Worst of all, nobody gives Nikki any attention! She's just an invisible shadow at home.

Nikki has to smile at school to make up for the down atmosphere at home. At school, though, Nikki can push aside that stab of worry or wave of sadness. She has to be up and bring laughter to her friends with the way she comically passes on her fat little plums of news.

Finally, she makes her way back to where she's supposed to be—World History class.

The teacher checks her watch and frowns as she accepts Nikki's pass. Nikki joins her friends to do some group work. Before she can dish, however, a student says: "Did you know that the passes from the office now have a time stamp? If you're more than five minutes late, you're in big trouble."

Uh-oh. Looks like Nikki just got caught, but punishment alone isn't going to help her. Someone needs to take time to inform her that:

 Laughing at a girl and gossiping about her behind her back is just as bad as actually saying something way mean to her face. ⁓ Carly, 16

Way mean is right. As if you don't have enough stress in your life already without having to worry about dealing with gossip and backstabbing! Every girl has gossiped or has been the victim of gossip at some time in her life; no one is innocent here. Just remember that gossiping is cowardly behavior that has no good outcome. The Gossip is seeking power, but you don't have to provide her with ammo!

> It's one thing to pick on someone behind her back, but it's another thing to say it to her face. I've had times where some girl will say something about me behind my back, but she doesn't have what it takes to say it to my face. But I don't worry about girls like her. They're just garbage to me. If I have something to say to someone, I say it to her face.
> ～Barbie, 16

Even if the victim tries to shrug it off, the Gossip and her buds can do some serious damage.

> There was this girl who would be so mean to me. Whenever she made a crude remark or gossip about me, one of my best friends who was in the class with me would just laugh like so loud, but it all went on behind my back. Later I found out about it. This lowered my self-esteem so much. I'm still having trouble. ～Carmen, 19

The Gossip is a smart cookie and she can sometimes be harder to spot than the Snob or "the Teaser" (discussed later). But her weapon is just as powerful, if not more so. Again, while her intentions may be misguided, try to remember that the Gossip has feelings just like you do and that intentionally hurting others is never cool. So, you can feel sorry for the Gossip, but first you should learn to protect yourself from her, so she can't get in your way!

Check out the quiz on the following page to find out if you're a target of the Gossip.

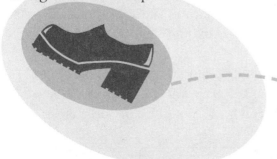

<FAST QUIZ>

Gossip Go-Around—Don't Let It Happen to You!

1. You've just been through a really heinous breakup with your longtime honey and you're feeling pretty low. You haven't seen a breakup this dramatic since Brittany and Justin split! During first period you take a bathroom break to clear your head. As you're washing your hands, the Gossip bounces through the door, notices you, and immediately begins to spout pseudo sympathy in order to get the scoop. You:

   a. Hesitate for a moment, then tell her everything. You're terrified that if you don't, she'll just make up lies about you, and then you'll feel even worse.

   b. Spill the beans immediately, basking in the glory of her attention for the moment and hoping you'll be able to wrangle an invite to sit with her crew at lunch. Attention is attention, no matter what form it comes in.

   c. Tell it all—and then some! The Gossip is like a walking tabloid and there is no such thing as bad publicity. Besides, spreading a little dirt around about your ex is the perfect revenge.

   d. Thank her for her concern, but tell her you'd rather keep it to yourself—your business is your business, and if you wanted the whole school to know, you'd tell them yourself.

2. You're at the salad bar at lunch, wishing you had taken your mom up on her offer for that PB&J, when the Gossip and a gaggle of her friends approach the bar, whispering and giggling. She asks you if you've heard the latest dirt on Melanie, a quiet girl you sometimes talk to in study hall. You:

   a. Listen and pretend to giggle along over Melanie's misery, even though you really don't want to. If you don't indulge the Gossip and her crew, you could be the next target.

b. Let them go ahead of you in line and anxiously join in the conversation—better to be part of the group than left out in the cold.

c. Dish, dish, dish! You eat up their gossip like it's today's lunch special and then share some of your own—nothing like a juicy rumor to spice up the school day!

d. Tell them no thanks. If you have any desire to know what's going on in Melanie's life, you'll ask her yourself.

3. You haven't even made it to your locker Monday morning when you realize that you're the latest target of the Gossip. You:

a. Stay as invisible as possible for the next few days—the Gossip and her group will find another victim soon enough.

b. Laugh along with them and try to make a joke of it—hey—gossip happens to everyone and you don't want people to think you're a bad sport.

c. Become a one woman *National Enquirer*—no way you're letting the Gossip ruin your rep without ruining hers right back. Never underestimating the power of the written word, you launch an e-mail rumor attack that will be legendary for years to come.

d. Hold your head high. You're as cool as a cucumber—you start walking along the red carpet with no time for busybodies. "No comment," you say to the Gossip and her group. Your life is your business and you're not interested in petty school politics.

4. The Gossip has started a rumor about a close friend of yours that you know is a total lie, and the whole school is buzzing with the news. When people ask you about it, you:

a. Don't say anything about it. You'd rather not get involved in such a mess, and your friend can take care of herself.

b. You feel a little guilty, but you tell every juicy detail you know. You'd hate for people to think that you're choosing sides.

c. Tell them every juicy detail you know—if gossip is a crime, then you're public enemy #1!

d. Tell them to get out of your face and leave your friend alone—don't they have anything better to do with their time?

Now it's time to find out how you did. Total up your answers.

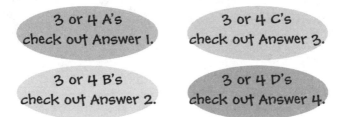

3 or 4 A's
check out Answer 1.

3 or 4 C's
check out Answer 3.

3 or 4 B's
check out Answer 2.

3 or 4 D's
check out Answer 4.

If you have a mixture of A's, B's, C's, and D's, look at all the answers. Obviously, there's a little bit of everything in you, which is great. Now can you work on getting a little more of that Answer # 4 attitude?

Answers

1. Class Coward

What's the deal here? You're so afraid to speak your mind that you're letting others walk all over you. Would saying what you think or feel really hurt that much? What are you so afraid of? You're giving way too much power to the Gossip when you should be giving that power to yourself. You should give it a try sometime—you'd be surprised at how good you'll feel opening up and saying what's on your mind. You'll gain the respect of your friends and your peers and, most importantly, yourself.

2. Attention Addict

You're so starved for attention from the Gossip and her gang that you'll do anything it takes to win their approval—even if it means mimicking the Gossip's bad behavior. If you aren't loyal to your friends when they need you, who is going to be left to be loyal to you? In the future when you are presented with any of these situations, try turning over a new leaf by being loyal to your friends and yourself—you may find that you enjoy the power of standing on your own rather than running with the pack.

3. Gossip Guru

Okay, so if gossiping were a class, you'd have a 4.0. But it's not! You got off-track here. You're in school to learn and become the best you can be and not to jibber-jabber about everybody's business but your own. Of course, it's great that you're the best snooper-outer and dirt-digger in your school, but what good do those traits do you? Besides your GPA, is there a Gossip Points Average at your school? If so, you're the valedictorian for sure.

4. Good Girl

The dish stops with you—good for you. You neither indulge in it nor listen to it. Hey, you like facts not figments, so everyone knows they can come to you for the truth—and nothing but the truth. There's nothing more powerful than being able to stop the Gossip at her own game. A definite score for you!

Gossip Smarts: What Should You Know about the Gossip?

However you get a grip on the Gossip, know that there's usually one or more in any group of girls, so how do you get those gossip smarts? Try the following:

1. Keep in mind that the Gossip is just starved for attention. When she grew up, she probably didn't get enough at home and maybe she still doesn't. Sure, she may attract lots of attention at school, but maybe there's nobody at her house to listen

to her. So understand what makes her tick, but don't give her the boot just yet.

2. The Gossip is frantic to make up for what she's missing—some importance, a feeling that she matters, and some super self-esteem. So she's grabbing at straws to get some. Understand that's what's driving her serious wish to dish, and give her some good news to spread.

3. Try to find the good in the Gossip. Most often she's a great communicator, really, but she hasn't found her niche yet. Otherwise, she'd use her talents for the good, not the bad.

Rapid Response: What You Should Do about the Gossip

Want some quick tips when faced with a gabby gossip? Next time you find yourself in a sticky situation, try one of these:

1. When you find out someone's been gossiping about you, say, "I heard what you're saying about me. Thanks for being such a good publicist, and I love your price. It's free."

2. Just smile and say something like, "You know what they say. 'Those who can, do. And those who can't, gossip about it.'"

3. You and your gal pals can dish some misinformation about yourself and record how this totally false rumor takes off around school like a swarm of bats out of Hades. Then tell the whole school about it or publish it in the school paper. The choice is yours. You are in charge!

And about that Ms. Backstabber? Well, first don't tell her any more personal stuff about yourself ever. Just cool it with her and rely on your *real* friends. Real friends are trustworthy, loyal, respectful, goofy with you when you feel like it, but most of all, safe. They are there 4 U. They're never dirt grabbers, secret blabbers, and backstabbers. Better not to have any "friends" like that.

First Person: What I Went Through—A Real Life Story

There's one girl in my neighborhood who has always done things in such a way that other girls found amusing. They'd laugh and talk and gossip about her behind her back all the time. It was like a sport or something. The worst thing they ever did to her was pretend to be her friend to her face. She never realized what they did to her. If she didn't do anything at all one day, they'd make up lies and spread them to all the kids.

During eighth grade, a few girls befriended the girl. They still talked junk behind her back. The girl was completely clueless and nobody ever told her the truth. The last week of school the girls pretended to get mad at the girl and didn't speak to her, and on the last day they planned to "jump" her. The girl's parents came to pick her up early and got there right as the fight was about to begin so, luckily, the girl was left unharmed.

Now that this girl is in high school, she found her own "crowd" and isn't picked on and when she is, she doesn't care. The other girls call her names like "slut, hoe, and bitch" when she walks by them, but it doesn't affect her anymore.

Just last week she won an award for having the highest grade point average in eleventh grade.

~Mya, 16

First Rate: Grade the Girls

A+ Awesome job! Pretty much on her own, this girl overcame the gossips and the backstabbers. That showed loads of courage. Getting called nasty names sure must have hurt as well as having to listen to the garbage the other girls dished out. But instead of letting it get her down in the dumps, this girl rose above it. The fact is, she got stronger and in the end she showed them all. While the gossips gabbed, this girl grabbed the opportunities. So she won, and the gossips were the losers, and sore ones at that. My only wish is that someone gets those mean girls to stop it!

 I think gossiping, spreading rumors, and namecalling in school should have consequences that are spelled out like in a student handbook. ~ Carla, 16

Dear Diary

And now it's time to fess up. Have you ever mindlessly repeated a juicy bit of gossip? Have you passed along some rumor and maybe even exaggerated it a little bit for that rush of power that comes from knowing something naughty about someone you don't think is so nice to begin with?

Or maybe you've heard or participated in gossip about a girl that you've always secretly envied and now this blemish on her record—ha ha!—makes you feel better because it means she's not so superior after all. Right?

Wrong. If you gossip about her and she doesn't about you, who's really superior? Hmm?

So now it's time to think about your actions. Honestly, have you ever gossiped to your heart's content? Have you parroted something you heard about another girl because it gave you a thrill to have some inside info? Think of a time that you gossiped about a friend or classmate and write a few paragraphs or pages about it in your journal.

Next, make a list of words that describe how you felt while you were doing it—powerful, popular, petty, guilty? And, remember, be honest! You don't have anything to lose here except maybe a bad attitude.

Look over the list and think about the words you chose to describe your feelings. What do they say about your personality? Now, imagine this scenario: You hear that the hottie you've been lusting after all year is interested in you. He's been asking some of your friends about you. When he asks what you're like, they tell him—using all of the words from your list. Yikes. How do you feel?

Next, write about a time that you were the subject of gossip or rumors in your journal. This time, make a list of words that describe how being the subject of gossip made you feel. Probably not too good, huh? Now make a list of the words that describe what you thought of the girls who spread the gossip. How many match with the first list that you made about yourself? Then compare your lists and think about the type of person you would like to be. Are you happy with what you've written down, or could you use some improvement?

We all know that the rumor mill at school changes faster than J-Lo at a concert, but should you find yourself the target of the Gossip and her group, just remember to hold your head up high and be proud of who you are. Don't let them get to you, and try to stay out of their range of fire. Better to devote your time to the friends who truly care about you!

Fab Fixes for Whatever Attitude Ails You

The urge to blab something juicy can creep into all of us once in a while. Gossiping about what hot movie stars are doing, wearing, and baring is harmless. After all, we all love to talk about who Eminem is dating or what happened last night on *Buffy*. Likewise, getting the scoop at school about who's seeing whom and who's wearing what can be a blast.

It's common (and fun!) to engage in this kind of chitchat sometimes. So if you do it rarely, good. But if it's an everyday occurrence, you'd better watch your back. This kind of gossipy attitude can easily morph into a bad habit that's hard to break. There may be days when your "blabbitude" takes over. Maybe you're ticked off that your best bud blew you off for her latest beau. Maybe you're seeking revenge on your little sister, so you jabber about her to your parents. Heck, maybe you just have a mean case of PMS. However, intentionally hurting others is very uncool.

So, if you find yourself feeling this way, you may be developing a "cattitude"! And to be catty means to be malicious, spiteful, cruel, and sneaky—none of these words sounds good, do they? So next time you feel your claws coming out, try one of the following tips.

Rx—Countering Cattitude

Do 3x a day:

1. No matter how tempting it may be, don't give in to that mean-speaking streak that surfaces every so often. You've got better things to do with your time! So, don't let yourself be a part of the rumor factory. When someone tells you some juicy gossip, say, "Aha, *verry* interesting." Then let it stop with you.

2. Spread nice rumors. That is, whenever you hear someone pass around something bad about a girl in your school, immediately pass around something way glowing about the same girl.

3. Go up to the girl who's being gossiped about and apologize to her. Make sure to tell her you don't believe a word of what's going around about her and that her life is no one else's business! Okay? A little bit of support goes a long way!

As for people gossiping about you, decide you won't let it get to you. You know you can ignore it, admit it's true, laugh it off, or best of all, be prepared for it. How? By rehearsing all kinds of zinger-type answers, writing them down first, and practicing them lots of times. Here are some more possible retorts to girls gossiping about you:

"Oh, if only you knew . . ."
"So what's your point?"
"If I could only talk . . ."
"What else is new?"

Most of all, get busy doing what you like to do so you'll be moving ahead instead of gossiping behind the backs of your girlfriends. Don't let any mean chicks get in your way!

The Bottom Line

Here's what you have to remember about the Gossip:

* She's dying for attention because she never got enough in the past or isn't getting enough now—at home or perhaps even at school. So she's trying to hog the limelight with her busy bee blabber.
* You really need to diss the dishing but not the source. Actually the girl who's the biggest gossip at school may be a verbal giant, but a self-esteem midget.
* Always picture a gossip as a popularity hound driven by attention hunger and sniffing for any juicy morsel to ease her hollow feeling. That way you know just how to act— you acknowledge her existence, understand her reasons, then rise above her. Far, far above! Wow!

Though you may gain fame and popularity at the time you're gossiping on other girls, you won't even be remembered in a few days or weeks. After graduation, your fame is over, only the pain that you gave goes on.
~ Hannah, 18

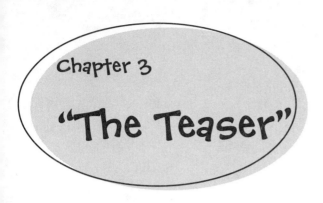

Chapter 3

"The Teaser"

Words to Live By: Violence of the tongue is very real—sharper than any knife. ~Mother Teresa

What Makes a Girl a Teaser?

 Many people use the phrase: Sticks and stones may break my bones, but words can never hurt me. Personally, I don't agree with that. At all! Words hurt people daily. Hurting words hurt so much. ~Amber, 15

In many ways, this mean queen—"the Teaser"—is much worse than the others. So many girls' lives have been ruined by her and her kind, and the worst thing is, she might not even know it! She could be your friend, your lab partner, or your neighbor. The fact is, she's always around, and she could be a good friend . . . that is, if you know how to handle her.

This girl can scare you, and yet, she's actually good bud material. That means, if she'd get help from someone—a classmate, a teacher, a coach, a mom or dad, or from *you!*—she can turn out to be your best gal pal.

Dear Dr. Erika:
It started last year. This girl who used to be my best friend started being ill with me. She called me Goodyear blimp and big drawers and all kinds of mean stuff. And she's way bigger than I am. And any time a boy looked at me and I started talking to him, she called him dopehead or

pothead. And behind my back this girl was and is even worse to this day. She talks junk about me to all the other girls, none of which is true.

I've tried to ignore her but that hasn't done any good. It's getting so that I don't want to go to school anymore. Really I don't know what to do . . .

~Tiana, 13

 Dear Dr. Erika:

Let me come right out and say it: My complexion isn't as good as other girls'. Used to be it was awful but now it's improving—a whole lot. Anyhow, when it was the pits nobody mentioned it, but now that it's looking okay, my friends have started picking on me. See, a long time ago, we had a lesson about some bird called a sandpiper and I got the best grade on a report I did. Ever since, the other girls in class called me Ms. Sandpiper. Except my best friend—or who I thought was my best friend—changed sandpiper to sandpaper. Because of my skin back then. Which is good now. Still, they call me Sandpaper wherever I go. And when we meet some new girls, like at church camp or wherever, my friend always introduces me as Sandpaper. I try to laugh it off, sure, and I try to call them names back but it hurts. It really does.

~Zoe Yang, 15

FYI

What is teasing, really, or "picking" as some girls call it?

How can you identify the Teaser and her close cronies, the Picker and the Name Caller? Are the Teaser's antics just cute chuckle-provokers? Is it just joking around? Or is there venom beneath her seemingly innocent veneer? While the Teaser's actions may seem at first to be fun and games, in time the teasing escalates until you just can't take it anymore.

 DO NOT PICK ON PEOPLE. You never know how a person feels about herself or how far from the edge she is. ~LaKeisha, 14

Sure thing—to start, you may laugh and go along with all her jokes and jeering, but eventually you may hear a warning bell going off in your head. First, maybe she gives you a funny nick-name, and you like it. You feel like she's adopted you as her friend. Next, maybe she rides you about the bad hair day you're having—heck, even you can admit when your 'do just won't coop-erate. But next, maybe she starts picking on your shoes or your clothes, or the way you speak, or the way you sign your name on your notes. And eventually, you find yourself flinching every time you pass her in the halls. You may feel hurt or even left out by her teasing, as if she's trying to make you feel bad for who you are. As if there was something really wrong with you!

It's time to stop this mean chick chatter! Sometimes it's subtle, but most often it shows itself in all kinds of serious needling and verbal bullying. That can range from someone calling you a bad name because of your looks, smarts, size, religion, ethnic back-ground, or because of your family, your friends, your background, your name, or the way you act, talk, or even walk. In other words, just about anything that might be a little different from others.

> These girls pick at my accent, you know? They say I talk "funny" but they do, too. My mom is from Miami and my dad is Puerto Rican. Of course that comes out in me. But these girls don't sound like the BBC either. So why are they making fun of me? ∼Teena, 18

The Teaser and her bosom buds, the Picker and the Name Caller, come in two basic formats:

1. Someone who's a friend who's just jealous of you and puts you down.
2. Someone you don't know that well who picks on you for seemingly no reason.

Yet whether they're close to you or not, it's hurtful to be teased. Oftentimes, this mean teasing is a way for someone who's hypercritical of you, or envious of you, to put you down while putting herself above you. The Teaser, as we said earlier, often doesn't even realize why she's doing it, only that she is slick and quick with a quip and likes to show off her so-called verbal superiority and glibness.

Who knows? Maybe she could be a real friend if she could find a beneficial outlet for her verbal gifts—like freestyle poetry or public debate. But for now, she's so fixated on her female classmates and spends lots of time and energy on verbally teasing and terrorizing them.

So if this is a "friend," who always seems to use words, names, phrases, or what have you to make you feel bad, cool it with this fool. She's no friend at all! Actually, she may be worse than foolish. She may do some real serious harm. If her teasing goes unchecked, it can lead to a heck of a lot of trouble—violence, total disaster, you name it.

Universal High School

What people call Gloria when they see her in action at home is "smart." That she is, in addition to being 5' 9", strong, athletic, and so pretty. Her dark brown hair is thick and slightly wavy, so she can wear it in a messy ponytail like it's in style right now at Universal High. Or she can just let it down and still it has so much body.

Of course, in addition to the great hair, she has a lovely face and light-olive skin that's smooth and silky. And those perfect teeth of hers! Still, Gloria thinks her hair is her best feature, and her girlfriends agree. But at home it's not about her hair.

Her mother died two years ago of breast cancer, and Gloria doesn't go a day without feeling an ache the size of a grapefruit inside her chest. Sometimes she thinks her rib cage is going to burst from all the pain in there. That's why she's glad she has all this lame housework to do, so she doesn't have time to think.

Now her three younger brothers and her dad are all her responsibility. Whew—just the laundry is enough to scare you. Some of Dad's uniform stuff alone . . . He's a firefighter. Talk about a constant mess. And that's not all. All the guys in the neighborhood come over and watch every game on ESPN with her dad. That means the house is a pigsty every day. What happened was that the guys started coming over after her dad started drinking. That was right before her mama passed away.

Anyway, Gloria is glad the guys are coming over because Dad stopped hitting the bottle, but man! What a noisy bunch—and all that backslapping and teasing. Some of it's kinda lewd and crude. They even pick on Gloria, her being the only female in the house. And sometimes her little brothers join in, too, even though she could kick their butts. They call her Little Mama, Mamita! Mamacita! But she's just fifteen and nobody's mama. They ask what the weather's like up there because she's taller than some of them. Or they tease her about her cooking and criticize her constantly, even her hair.

Even though she wants to explode, she doesn't pick back at them—that will just make it worse. Still, they say, "Whatsa matter? Why aren't you like your papa? He's the funniest guy in Chicago."

Yeah, right. Maybe before Mama died. But now, when he's in his room late at night and thinks everyone's asleep, Gloria can hear him crying. Gloria doesn't cry but she used to, not that it helped. But now she's just angry—not real angry and not all the time, but a little some of the time. Most of the time! These anger fits grab a hold of her mostly at school when she sees all these other slick chicks who have it sooo easy. All they have to do is go to class and study, then home to rest, recoup, relax. Chill at will—Heck, Gloria wishes she could do likewise just one blankety-blank time!

As she hits the front entrance of school this day, she's actually feeling pretty good. She's already done two loads of laundry and parried with the big joker next door. "Hey, squirt," she says to a tiny girl she sees. "Why don't you eat something once in a while, you skinny minnie?" she snaps at another. "What? You wearing a mop today?" she shouts and chuckles as she sees a third girl who has an unfortunate haircut. "Nice wig, loser."

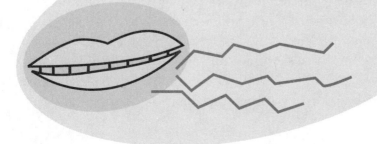

By the time Gloria enters first period class, she's teased a dozen girls, some of whom are actually her friends. So what? It's just for fun, right? If those prissy chicks can't take the heat, they should get the heck out of her way. And the same goes for her friends. If they're such good friends, why do they have to take everything so personally? Like Amy, who suddenly stopped talking to her because one day she made a crack about Amy's outfit. Why can't her friends understand that she's just teasing? After all, she has to put up with the same thing every night at home.

Knowing Gloria's background, perhaps it's understandable that Gloria has a tendency to pick on other girls at school. We can understand it, and perhaps at some point, we can forgive her for it. Even though we may not like what she does. We never like it. And knowing there are reasons for the actions of the Teaser doesn't necessarily lessen the pain.

In fact, teasing can have tragic consequences. Though most girls are stronger than they're given credit for (even if they won't let them play football!), almost no one is strong or tough enough to tolerate constant teasing. Mean words can cut to the marrow. Actually, they can be sharper than a blade. You might think to endure it is to cure it, but that's not the answer.

Besides, the more you put up with it, the bolder these mean taunts and teases can get. Instead of teasing less, the Teaser just keeps picking and taunting other girls, getting more boisterous, biting, and bitter with each passing day.

Does any of this sound familiar to you? Are you a victim of the Teaser, or perhaps you're one yourself? Then remember, teasing is *not okay*—no matter what. So under no circumstances must you tolerate cruel, racial, sexist, or homophobic teasing of any kind, not of yourself nor of any other girl. You have the power to put a stop to it. Right now.

 People have always told me to do unto others as you would like them to do unto you. So I try hard to be nice to everyone. —Taryn, 14

<FAST QUIZ>

The "Teaser Test"—How Well Do You Cope?

So, it's time for a fast quiz:

1. You've recently made friends with the new girl at school. At first she seems cool, and it seems like she's potential best bud material. But lately she's been treating you badly, calling you names and stuff. You're starting to feel really weird around her, and you don't know what to do. Then, finally, she takes it too far and says some really embarrassing stuff to you at lunch right in front of your crush. You:

   a. Try as best you can to keep your cheeks from flushing and wait for the torture to end. If you keep quiet, maybe she'll cut it out.

   b. Laugh louder at yourself than the others. After all, if your crush sees you've got such a charming sense of humor, maybe he'll ask you out.

   c. Tell her she's not funny and point out that huge hunk of spinach between her two front teeth. That'll fix her.

   d. Let her know that she's pushing it—and try and steer the subject away from any potentially embarrassing subject matter. Later, when you're alone, you'll have a talk with her and let her know that you don't consider her actions acceptable.

2. On the bus ride home, the Teaser and her gang have been picking on a girl who's really quiet and always sits alone. Each day, she bolts off the bus with tears in her eyes. You:

   a. Turn up your headphones and ignore the situation. It's a jungle out there, and you'd rather not get involved.

   b. Snag a seat next to the Teaser and try to join in—better to be the teaser than the teased! Besides, that girl they're teasing is a nobody anyway.

c. Carefully plan your attack. You can't stand a chick with a bad 'tude, and the Teaser and her friends have got it! You'll teach them a lesson and maybe that other girl will be able to leave the bus with a smile.

d. Try snagging the seat next to the girl who's being picked on and talk to her—there's safety in numbers, and you're not so concerned with what the Teaser and her group have to say. If you show them they're not bugging you, they'll probably back off in a few days, anyway.

3. For some reason, you just can't get the Teaser and her friends off your back! Every day for the past week, they've been giggling, snickering, and saying stuff as you pass by the second-floor water fountain, their usual hangout. To make matters worse, you found an "anonymous" note in your locker this morning that reiterates all of the things they've been teasing you about, written in the Teaser's conspicuous handwriting. You:

a. Choose another route so you don't have to pass by them in the hall—you're afraid you'll burst into tears if they say anything to you.

b. Spend the weekend trying to fix whatever it is they've been picking on—hair, makeup, clothes, whatever. If you can fix whatever it is they hate about you, maybe they'll stop bothering you.

c. Gather all of your best girl buds together and write a rebuttal note that points out everything that is wrong with the Teaser and her group. Deliver it to them by hand along with your best catty comment. What the heck—it's best to fight fire with fire.

d. Take a strong stance. You're a strong girl, so look them in the eye and say, "Is that the best you can do? Getting your kicks out of teasing people? I really feel sorry for you." Then walk off with your head held high, on to more important things. Sure, it may take a lot of courage to do that, but you've got it. Besides, the feeling of relief that comes afterward is even better than the best chocolate milkshake (well, almost!).

4. You're in yearbook class, which meets after school, and you just handed in a layout to a girl who is two grades ahead of you. She takes one look at your work, breaks out laughing, and calls the rest of the journalism crew together, pointing out every mistake you made. You:

a. Sit there listening to all the cruel stuff and suck it in like a vacuum cleaner. Or you nod like a bobble head doll, saying, "You're so right, I'm so dumb, this was stupid—will you give me another chance please?" You bow and scrape and stammer, then sneak into the hall and wipe off your watery eyes, vowing to somehow drop this class.

b. Say, "Oh you're so right! I don't know why I never thought of that before. I can change it if you want. Maybe I can model it after one of your layouts? You're so talented!"

c. Say, "Listen, bigmouth, my layout rocks. Maybe if you spent more time studying and less time brushing your hair, you wouldn't have flunked your trig exam, so back off!"

d. Say, "Thanks for the comments. I know you're trying to help, but I got these ideas from the award-winning yearbook that the school across town has done. It's time we updated the dinosaur designs we've always used and put our school on the map. Look, I've got to run—swim team meets in fifteen minutes. Call or e-mail me later. I've got this fantastic idea for a cover!"

Now it's time to find out how you did. Total up your answers.

3 or 4 A's
check out Answer 1.

3 or 4 C's
check out Answer 3.

3 or 4 B's
check out Answer 2.

3 or 4 D's
check out Answer 4.

If you have a mixture of A's, B's, C's, and D's, look at all the answers. Obviously, there's a little bit of everything in you, which is great. Now can you work on getting a little more of that Answer #4 attitude?

Answers

1. Quiet Riot

Hey, girl! Hold that head up as high as you can! Since when does ignoring a problem make it go away? And how does running from a confrontation solve anything? That tactic may work for that stubborn zit that appeared on your chin at totally the wrong moment, but it won't work for the Teaser and her gang! There's nothing wrong with staying out of the way of trouble. The Teaser is certainly troublesome, but there is something to be said for standing up for yourself. So do it. Quit stalling and make a promise not to always flee or act like a flea. You're not a doormat they can use to stomp on and wipe their feet. Think of all the good things you have in your life and remember, this is just a brief moment in time. If you don't start making a difference for yourself now, how will you ever become the superstar you were meant to be?

2. Teaser Pleaser

You're letting the other girls label you and make fun of you. Why? What they're really doing is labeling themselves. You have so much potential to do great things. Why would you try to change who you are because of the whims of the Teaser?

You spend too much time trying to adapt yourself to suit the Teaser's tastes, and let's face it, if she had any taste at all, she wouldn't spend so much time putting you down. Stop being a Teaser Pleaser! Instead, try doing something that you love in order to please yourself. You'll soon find yourself walking through life with a whole new outlook.

3. Queen of the Hill

You're not afraid to put the smack down on the Teaser when she's getting on your case or the cases of other girls. You have low tolerance for ignorance, and there's no way you'll ever let the Teaser feel like she's on top when you're around. But don't go patting yourself on the back just yet. Beating the Teaser at her own game a time or two will definitely help put her in her place, but you're not here to stir up trouble. Sometimes challenging the Teaser stirs up more trouble than it's worth.

> The main place where kids are most commonly picked on and teased is the bus. My sister is heavy and last year on the bus she was called "Piggy." I didn't appreciate it and started picking on the little girl who started the mess. Only I told the truth. She is a spoiled brat who's going to end up dropping out of school. She's only twelve, already talking about sex, and is getting worse every day! ～Anna, 15

4. Head of the Class

Okay, so you admit it. On a bad day, the Teaser definitely gets to you. But it's okay. You've got enough class to know when to stand up for yourself and when those boots were made for walkin'! Maybe you can take your smarts a step further, if you wish. Why not try to stop the tease sleaze at other girls' expense at your school? There are plenty of things you can do to stop it . . . just wait and see!

Teaser Smarts: What Should You Know about the Teaser?

While the Teaser and close cronies can have complex reasons for acting like they do, you run across them in just about any class or group of girls. So what should you know about the Teaser?

★ The Teaser feels bad about herself: Maybe she's not getting any respect at home, or nobody has ever made her feel worthwhile, or she's constantly teased and criticized herself. As a result, she's trying to drag you down in the gutter where she feels she is.

★ Remember, by belittling something in you or about you, or about your background, your family, and your friends, she wants to climb out of the hole she feels she's in.

★ But even the worst Teaser, Picker, or Name Caller can break her mean habits. It may take some time, but if you feel like it, try to befriend the Teaser. Maybe with your help she will improve.

Rapid Response: What You Should Do about the Teaser

So now that you know about the Teaser, what can you do about her? Try these:

1. The first time someone teases you, say, "Funny, ha ha ha," but with a serious face. The second time say, "You said the exact same thing yesterday. What's wrong? Are you okay?" Act real concerned. The third time, calmly record on paper what's being said, word for word, and by whom, when, and where. When someone asks, "What're you doing?" you reply, "I'm documenting what's going on. Just in case this ends up in court. My dad says, 'You always have to have the facts first.'" This might get some laughs, but it will stop most of the serious teasing on the spot. Trust me.

2. If the Teaser keeps it up, carry a small tape recorder and ask the mean chick: "Would you mind repeating what you just said? I just want to make sure I have you quoted accurately." Then tape her slurs, bad words, and names, whatever she has to say.

3. But if the teasing persists to a point where you really can't take it anymore and your smart girl tactics aren't working as you thought they would, maybe it's time to share your problems with someone else who can help. Take the evidence to someone you trust—a teacher, a guidance counselor, or even

your mom or dad. Pretend you're a lawyer and think of it as a case you're going to handle. But don't bluff—really resolve to solve it.

Whenever someone calls me a name, I just say, "Stop it." If they do it again, I repeat, "Stop it!" The third time I'm either in the office or talking to the guidance counselor about it, okay? ～Debbie, 16

In general, it helps to work with your class council or the student government or through the PTA. Just get out some basic facts about how your classmates should act. Respect is key. And you should be proud of being different.

You shouldn't tease other girls just because they are different. We are all different in some way. ～Natalia, 17

So often in the news, there are reports of girls suffering emotional and physical problems and stress from constantly being picked on and teased by other girls. All I can say is, "Stop it!" ～Ellyn, 14

But should the teasing atmosphere at your school continue, there are things you can do to tease-proof your school. Organize a group of girls who are sick of the teasing and namecalling and the consequences.

Don't ever pick on someone and call her a name. It's so cruel. And it could be the very thing that pushes her <u>over the edge</u> of the cliff. ～Shanika, 15

Choose a cool name for your group—any updated term for the Avengers or the Mod Squad will do. Brainstorm, then find a teacher you're close to who will sponsor your group. Think of yourselves as the Charlie's Angels of your school—battling evil in whatever form it comes. You can plan weekly meetings, get speakers to come, and maybe even network with other high schools.

 I think sadly everyone has experienced some kind of teasing or taunting from kids their age. I have been a victim of it. I still get nightmares. ⁓ Sonya, 19

Again, letting teasing happen to someone around you and not stopping it just isn't cool. Take a look at the examples below. If Rose and Julia still remember the incidents, you can bet the victims remember them, too.

 I remember last year at an assembly, the whole school was in the gym and this girl came in walking kind of strange and the whole school went into an uproar of laughter and rude comments. And they kept rehashing this for weeks. Sometimes I wonder how that girl felt and whatever happened to her. ⁓ Rose, 15

What good is it to think *later* about how embarrassed a girl who was teased might have felt? No good at all! For even though the girl may have acted like it didn't bug her, we know it did.

There was this girl in English class who had long and wild hair. One girl called her "Mop Top" and we all started laughing. Sure it was funny, but nobody thought how embarrassed the girl might have been. ⁓ Julia, 16

Labels are for soup cans and sunscreens, not for people. By labeling others around you, you aren't giving them a fair shake because you aren't letting yourself see them for who they really are. Instead, you're creating a false image of them. Picture branding cattle with a hot poker. Well, that's the way it feels to a girl who gets called an awful name day after day after day.

Don't call people names. Please! It can lead to injuries or maybe deaths because everyone can't take mean jokes. ～Andrea, 18

First Person: What I Went Through—A Real Life Story

When I was in eighth grade, there was a tiny girl who was cross-eyed and wore thick glasses. She was always so sad because the other girls picked on her about her glasses: "Four Eyes, Four Eyes!" they said, or "Man, she's blind as a bat!" She was horrified to go to school every day and face these cruel girls. She would cry and tell her parents she felt bad so she wouldn't have to go to school.

This continued for a couple of years until it got so bad that the tiny girl cried at school. This made the bullies tease her even worse. She had very few friends that were really nice to her because those mean girls would pick on them, too.

Then in tenth grade the girl asked her mother to get her contact lenses to help solve her problem.

Today this girl is one of the best, most popular cheerleaders in the school. She overcame her tormentors and the tough issues she had to deal with every day in middle school. Quite a few younger girls look up to her now because she found it inside of herself to forgive those girls who had hurt her so badly for so long. She thinks that the things she went through have made her a better person in the long run, and she never picks on anyone because of something they can't help.

I'm just so proud of this girl who just happens to be my younger sister.

～*Jennifer, 18*

First Rate: Grade the Girls

A+ This girl persevered, and didn't let teasing ruin her life. Instead, she became stronger. I'm sure having a big sister like Jennifer helped her, too. Can you think of someone from your school who has overcome a similar obstacle? Who knows, maybe that person was even you! Keeping positive, even in the face of hard situations, can help you to survive and thrive. Mean teasing hurts, but just try to remember that those cruel words only have meaning if you let them. The Teaser is using these tactics to make herself feel better, but you don't have to let her get you down.

 Is it really worth breaking down someone's self-esteem and confidence just so you can look big and bad for a few minutes? ～ Vickie, 17

Dear Diary

Now it's time to think about what you can do to prevent teasing. For starters, there is no greater comfort (not even your favorite blue jeans!) than knowing you are not alone. Teasing has been around for eons, and it will probably never stop completely. However, you can use your girl power to give support to your friends and classmates. Try this little exercise below. You can do it just for yourself, or, if you want to, you can share it with others. It's your call. So, take a survey of ten, twenty, or even one hundred girls in your school. Ask them if they have ever been the victims of teasing. Then ask them how it made them feel.

Why interview one hundred?

So you can get a simple percentage. If sixty-seven girls tell you they have been teased, you can then state that 67 percent of the female students you interviewed have been teased. Then get your creative juices flowing. Write an article about teasing and how it has affected you and the girls in your school. Write as if you're a magazine reporter and your words will reach thousands of people. First, start with a rough draft in your trusty journal, but just think: Wow! How many girls could be helped this way? If you like what you've come up with, maybe you can post it on a Web site or publish it in your school paper, or maybe even send it off to your favorite magazine. If not, you can keep it for yourself to read a few years from now or maybe even to share with your own children someday.

 Being called a name and made fun of is the worst feeling in the world. It hurts! ~ Carinna, 16

Fab Fixes for Whatever Attitude Ails You

Have you ever teased anyone? A classmate, a friend, your little sister? If so, you did the normal thing. We all like to do a little kidding now and then. I kid you not!

 Some girls pick on others because they were picked on when they were younger. It's a little like revenge. ~ Cora, 17

So, if the kidding is good-natured, infrequent, and nobody minds, then that's okay. It's always fun to laugh and kid with friends—it can even be a form of affection.

But keep in mind that the line between harmless kidding and hurtful teasing is a fine one, so be sure to watch yourself. If you find that you've been teasing in a sarcastic or negative way, maybe it's because you're developing a negative attitude about yourself. Just because you're having a rotten day doesn't mean that you should try to make others have a rotten day, too. So whenever you are tempted to show a nasty attitude, in other words a Nasty-tude, that makes you say stuff that's rude, do something to counteract it.

Rx—Nixing Nasty-tude

Do immediately when you feel a case of Nasty-tude coming on:

1. Turn the nasty into nice. Rather than letting nasty words come out of your mouth, make it a point to compliment those around you. Do it more than once—you'll be amazed at the response.

2. If you do find yourself with a bad case of Nasty-tude, apologize immediately to anyone you've picked on. Tell her you're sorry and you won't do it again. And then mean it.

3. Whenever you feel the urge to tease, immediately do something that makes *you* feel better, like taking a quick walk, stretching way up by standing on your toes and seeing how far you can reach, doing a crazy dance step, breathing in way deep, saying a favorite word three times, like "love-love-love." Whew. By then, your mean gene will have taken a hike.

The Bottom Line

The bottom line about teasers is to remember the following:

* Deep down the Teaser isn't pleased with herself, not at all. That's why she wants to spread some unpleasantness your way whenever she can.

* Don't forget, the Teaser is insecure. Her cure for that is trying her best to make you and others insecure, too. Don't take the Teaser's biting barbs as personal. From this moment on, put a shield around yourself that deflects her verbal arrows. This shield comes from your know-how, which gives you power.

* Help other girls around you arm themselves with this shield, too. Do it as soon as you observe another girl getting teased, because often you might not get a second chance in this. And you don't want to carry the burden of not having done something—small or big—to stop the verbal bullying when you could have. Remember, the time to stop it is now. Tomorrow may be too late.

 When the taunting and teasing never stop, girls get <u>so</u> angry and their frustration grows and grows. As a result, they might do something real real dumb.
~Jenna, 16

So whenever there's a culture of the vultures (mean girls dominating the scene) at your school, closing your eyes and shutting your ears is no way to solve the problem—for yourself or for others. You must be courageous. Be the heroine for the underdog. Be as strong as you can, and right the wrong.

One thing to remember is that the girls you act nasty to are usually some of the nicest girls you could meet and would give you the shirts off their backs. Tormenting other girls therefore deletes another terrific person from the list of your potential friends. ～Dianne, 18

Chapter 4

"The Bully"

Words to Live By: You cannot hate other people without hating yourself. ~Oprah Winfrey

What Makes a Girl a Bully?

Once the bullies push a girl to the edge, she has a wish for revenge, or more commonly, an urge to escape. She wants the pain to end one way or another. She does what she can to make it stop. Make it end. Please God, make it end! ~Kerri, 16

She's defiant, outspoken, and tough. She may run alone or with her pack, and she seems to get her kicks out of being cruel to smaller or weaker people. You've probably seen her—throwing hateful stares to classmates, whispering threats as you walk past her in the halls, or maybe even hitting or pushing you when she thinks no one else is looking. On the surface, this is truly a mean chick! You've just encountered . . . the Bully. But read on, for this chick who's so tough on the outside might not really be what she seems.

Dear Dr. Erika:
I hate school. Because . . . well, every time I pass by this tall mean-looking girl in the hall, she punches me hard—I got the bruises to show you. But nobody listens to me. My mother, she says to just take another stairway and then what happens? My teacher writes me up because I'm late. And I don't even know the girl! Why is she so mean?

~Anika, 16

Dear Dr. Erika:

I've always been good at sports, and I've played on a team at school since seventh grade with the big girls. Really, this is no brag. But lately I'm beginning to dread going to practice. There is another girl my age who's really tall and she's mean. Not when the coach is looking—oh no, then she's all goody-goody. But when he steps out of the gym to get his mail from the main office and we have the run of the place to ourselves, then she intentionally hits me with her elbow. Or she runs into me. She always grins from ear to ear—excuse me, excuse me!—but I'm not fooled. I know she's trying to hurt me till I quit. So maybe that's what I should do, but I love the game of basketball. I mean just look at those Duke University girls, how they do. That's what I see when I close my eyes. But then I feel all those bruises and worse. Why does this tall girl hate me so?

~Charlotte, 14

FYI

Now this is one scary chick. Her actions ruin school for so many girls by haunting the hallways and staircases, just waiting to cause trouble. Even if you try to avoid her, if you're the target of the Bully, it's inevitable that you'll run into her, whether you want to or not. The Bully has it in for other girls, that's for sure! You've probably experienced her in action—cursing out other girls, "accidentally" bumping into them or making them drop their books, or stealing their stuff. When confronted by a teacher, the Bully says with a saccharine smile, "Oh, I just borrowed that stuff. No big deal."

It's not hard to figure out that the Bully is just trying to hurt you. Maybe you don't even like going to school anymore because you're constantly on the lookout for her. She and her gang can pop up everywhere—in the halls, stairways, and the bathroom—and it's never good news when you spot her. There will always be some violent acts, small or large, or the threat of it hanging in the air when the Bully is roaming around.

Of all of the types of mean chicks, the Bully is probably the toughest one to handle because she uses physical violence. Yes, violence! No matter what physical things she's doing to you—from a small shove in the hallway to a nearly invisible punch on the arm—it's violence and it's wrong! Violence in girls can have many different causes, and those causes can be really hard to put into words. Your job isn't to find out what causes the violence, but to not let the Bully get in the way of your happiness or peace of mind. As you've probably figured out by now, there are no magic words that will make the Bully go away, no happy "after school special" ending to her story. But there are a few things that you can do to empower yourself. The list below provides three things you can do to handle this behavior. And it's not as complicated as you might think, but it does require you to be brave. Okay, here goes:

> 1. Stop being a victim.
> 2. Help others stop being victims.
> 3. Do your best to speak out and stop the terrorism that's ruining school for so many girls.

So remember these simple words: No more! It's got to stop. And it will—with you.

Bullying breeds bullying and violence breeds violence. Once it's tolerated, it only gets worse. If the behavior of the Bully and her crew is left unchecked, you might even see some of the girls from previous chapters—the Snob, the Gossip, and the Teaser— pick up bullying behavior.

 There are so many girls who are the victims of bullying peers. It often happens after school, that they get scratched or pinched for no reason except just being there. ～Leila, 14

The Bully is a real problem in just about every school. And even though many schools are now aware of the problem, it goes on not only during regular class time but also after school when girls participate in all their fun extracurricular activities.

But, whoa! There's no fun with the Bully around. Not when you have to take the long way to your destination, say, the gym where a meeting is being held to plan floats for the Homecoming Parade. How can you enjoy going to a club meeting when you are scared you might run smack into the Bully and her bad buds? Nowhere on the school grounds is safe!

Many bullies may have a background of dysfunction or violence at home. In other words, something went wrong with their lives or families early on. So they've learned to be cruel or lash out at others as a form of self-defense. Because they have been injured, they want to injure you. Bullies often come from homes where they're cursed at or beaten, or simply ignored.

Throughout my life there have been many times that I looked down on myself and cried. This was all the cause of other girls bullying me. They pushed me or elbowed me aside every chance they got. I don't know how many times I ended up with a bruise. ∼ Niqua, 14

Universal High School

Kelli is a pretty sixteen-year-old girl, 5' 7", with stunning blue eyes and light brown hair cut in a cool short style so she can wear it spiky or plain, depending on her mood. Everybody knows her because she's a major female jock, in other words a star athlete. She holds the record for most points scored in a girls' basketball game, and that's just one of her sports.

But what people don't know about Kelli would surprise them. Kelli's parents died in a car crash when she was just two years old. She spent the next five years of her life being shuffled around from one relative to another. So after she had made the rounds, she ended up in a foster home where there was a bunch of older girls. She felt alone but at least she had something she clung to— her new little puppy. Was it ever cute. But whenever the foster parents didn't let the older girls have their way, they kicked the puppy.

It turns out the foster parents were allergic to dogs, so they gave the puppy away, despite Kelli's begging and pleading. That's when the older girls started kicking Kelli. Nothing serious at first, only a kick or two in the shin under the table at supper. When the foster mother asked Kelli why her legs were so bruised, she wanted to speak up. But the bigger girls raised a fist behind the foster mother's back.

So Kelli shrugged off the pain. The kicking escalated to outright beatings, which wouldn't have been so bad if Kelli could've cried out. But there was always the threat of more beatings, so she could never tell anyone.

All this stuff happened years ago, of course. The older girls ran away, but Kelli stayed put and tried hard never to think about what she went through. Except there's this anger burning in her from way back that's never been released, never been dealt with.

Of course, Kelli's life is better now. She's at Universal High and making pretty good grades. She has her own crew—girls like herself who came from tough situations, too, and still made it. Not one wimp or wuss among them. No, sir. And they rule the school. No other girl better mess with them, and everyone knows it.

Kelli is the boss of the gang, natch. Every day, on her way to practice, she clatters down the stairs, scattering all of the girls who happen to be walking up, just to keep up her image. She shoves them aside, and if any nosy newcomer gapes at her, she knocks them way out of her way. She smiles at the rush of power she feels as she watches them cower away from her. All these lame sissies, she thinks. She wishes she could get rid of them all—what a bunch of wallflowers, silly cutesy-pies, girly-girly gals, yikes! With their makeup mess, red fin-gernail claws, and their high heels and—sheesh!

Kelli's on the varsity basketball team and doing real well. But the coach keeps warning her about not getting into fights at prac-tice. Even though she's the star player, the fighting is affecting her record. Coach has been cutting her slack, but lately Kelli has the feeling that she's been pushing it too far. She almost got in major trouble for that fistfight in the lunchroom the other day, and it almost cost her playing in the game this weekend!

As she waits for practice, Kelli decides to start on her English homework. It's a "free write," meaning she gets to pick her own topic. Kelli enjoys the assignment, describing in vivid detail that last basketball game when she scored 24 points. Basketball is her passion, and she is surprised how easily the words come out. As she finishes, however, Kelli's smile turns to a frown. At the bottom of the page, she scribbles in the smallest handwriting possible: P.S. Sometimes I want to kill myself! And then quick as a wink, she erases it.

Even though she loves basketball, Kelli's anger issues are in danger of keeping her from playing. While basketball is a great way for Kelli to work off some of her anger, taking it out on girls in the hallways or on the court is not cool. Luckily, Kelli has her coach watching out for her. But not all girls have a parent or teacher or coach keeping tabs on them.

> Usually, I like to make my presence as peaceful as pos-sible, but sometimes I do get a real urge to hurt other girls in some way either by kicking them or slapping them. But what I have to do is overcome those hateful feelings.
> ～Jana, 15

Jana is right to recognize that she needs to overcome those feelings, but that can't always be done alone. Some girls have so many things to deal with that getting at the root of their anger, which is often the basis of physical bullying, can be tough if they try to do it without getting outside help. Indeed, if you or someone you know is trying to tackle feelings of anger that don't go away, it may be best to seek help from adults whom you trust. It's natural to be angry at times, like when you have the kind of day where you miss the school bus, forget your biology homework, and halfway through your first period your hair decides to freak out.

But when that anger becomes uncontrollable or overshadows everything else in your life, it's best to turn to someone who can help.

 Every girl takes her anger out in different ways — some in money, some in food, and some in beating up on other girls. — Veronica, 17

True, and since they're so many angry girls around, you need a quick way to find out if you're at risk in your school.

‹FAST QUIZ›

Bully Battles—Are You a Victim?
Time for a fast quiz:

1. The school cafeteria is jam-packed. Because of an assembly earlier, all grade levels have the same lunch hour on this day, which means there are no empty tables left for latecomers. You've managed to snag one of the last remaining tables for you and your friends, who are still in the lunch line. But the Bully and her crew decide they want the table. She marches up to it, kicks your chair, and snaps, "Move it. Now!" You:

    a. Get the heck out of there as quickly as you can! Without making eye contact, you slink away to find your friends and explain what happened. Maybe you can sit on the floor or squeeze in with another table.
    b. Yell, "Teacher, teacher, I am being victimized by a bully and my self-esteem is being irreparably damaged! This is

a direct violation of our school's 'Zero Tolerance' policy. Fix this problem or I'm calling Daddy's lawyer!" That should get the attention of the teachers on lunch duty and make the Bully disappear in a hurry.

c. Say, "No problem, I was just leaving." As you stand up, you "accidentally" overturn your lunch tray and dump the remaining cafeteria gruel all over the Bully.

d. Say, "I see that you're upset and confused. You know, I think that the guidance office has an after-school anger management program for people like you. It's not good to let all that bitterness build up inside—first thing you know, you've got an ulcer, then you're going down with a heart attack—who knows? Why don't you go check it out? Meanwhile, this is my seat and I'm not leaving. You're dismissed . . . want a tatertot for the road?"

2. You've been assigned a research topic on Shakespeare and you're in the library, just "Googling" away. There are only a dozen computer stations, but your teacher posted a schedule, and this is your allotted time. The Bully strides in, hovers over you, and snaps, "Outta my way. I got stuff to do." You:

a. Flutter away as fast as your espadrilles will take you, losing all of your research in the process. The Bully always gets her way, no matter what, so it's easier just to let her take over. You can come back during study hall or lunch and start over again.

b. You're practically a computer genius, and you know the Bully hardly knows her password. This is your chance to finally get on her good side. Not only do you graciously give up your computer, but you offer to help her do her research . . . and her report.

c. Tell her you'll get up when your time is up and not a minute sooner, then turn your back and continue with your work. You even stay ten minutes past your allotted time, just to mess with her. As an added bonus, before you sign off, you make sure to jam the printer and misplace the mouse. Heck, she never makes *your* life easy—and revenge is so sweet!

d. Say in a firm, loud voice: "Please, don't interrupt me again!" Then go on with your work. You never knew there was so much stuff about Shakespeare on the Net, and some of it is even interesting! With any luck, you could have your research done in one shot, leaving more time for fun. When the Bully hovers over you, glaring, you point to the posted schedule and say: "If you want the schedule changed, why don't you see Mrs. Smith? She's right over *there*."

3. After school you're on your way to an important meeting to plan the annual school fair. You've been looking forward to serving on the committee all year. Bummer that you run into the Bully on the staircase, and she's in the mood for trouble. She blocks the staircase leading down to the walkway that connects the main building to the gym. You:

a. Try to smile and move around her, but she just won't let you by. You look around, hoping someone else will come into the staircase so she'll have to move, but no one shows. Finally, you turn and walk back up the steps, out the doors, and head home. It's just not worth the trouble. Besides, there will be tons of girls at the meeting anyway, and they don't need you and your silly suggestions. No one will even miss you.

b. Compliment her on her outfit, haircut, shoes, whatever. After all, they say flattery will get you everywhere. Once you get her talking about herself, you can slip by, down the stairs, and safely to your meeting. Besides, if you score points with her now, maybe she won't bug you so much in the future.

c. Okay, that's it! You've had a lousy day as it is, and you don't need the Bully getting in your face and making it worse. So you get in her face instead. Your momma didn't raise no scaredy-cat, not by a long shot. Too bad a teacher breaks it up before things get ugly, but you think: Let the word go out to everybody—don't tread on me!

d. You calmly assess the situation. Chances are, if you stand your ground, she'll let you by. You meet her gaze directly, and say, "Excuse me," making sure your tone is polite yet firm. If she still won't let you by, you make a choice. You can continue to confront her in a mature and confident way, willing to face whatever may happen, or you can turn around and take a different, bully-free route to the meeting.

4. You're at the bus parking lot waiting for your bus when the Bully and her gang show up and "accidentally" bump into you. You:

a. Apologize and move a few steps away from them. When that doesn't work, you slink back into the building and call your mom for a ride. Public transportation isn't what it used to be, and you don't mind waiting two hours for your mother to come. It's a good time to catch up on your math work.

b. Laugh along and try to join in their conversation. Maybe if you can join in on their banter, they'll include you instead of being rude to you.

c. Yell, "Do it again, I dare you!" as loud as you can so everyone around you stops and stares. The Bully looks startled and takes a step back. While you have everyone's attention, you yell again, "Yeah, that's right, back away! It's what you do best anyway!" Other kids around you look frightened, but you know the Bully well enough to know she's all talk. You'll show her who the boss of this school is—and it sure ain't her!

d. Throw her a sideways glance and step quietly away from the Bully and her friends. You act like it was an accidental bumping, but you still move away from the Bully and near a teacher or supervisor. If the same thing happens again, you'll probably take more serious steps, but for now, it's better to leave it alone.

Now it's time to find out how you did. Total up your answers.

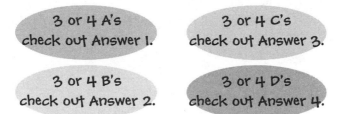

3 or 4 A's
check out Answer 1.

3 or 4 C's
check out Answer 3.

3 or 4 B's
check out Answer 2.

3 or 4 D's
check out Answer 4.

If you have a mixture of A's, B's, C's, and D's, look at all the answers. Obviously, there's a little bit of everything in you, which is great. Now can you work on getting a little more of that Answer #4 attitude?

Answers

1. Boo-hoo Baby

We know the Bully can be scary, but you're letting her control your life, and that's holding you back from doing what you want to do when you want to do it. Why let the Bully dictate your actions? She's just a boil on the student body, and she's the one who needs to shape up or ship out, not you. So, get on with your life and get on the ball. You have the right to walk anywhere you like.

2. Wimpy Wanda

Who are you, someone's slave? Stop kowtowing to every whim of the Bully. By doing what she says, you're making the situation worse for you and for other girls. Your fearful actions are enabling the Bully to keep on bullying, and that's not cool. No matter what you may think, the Bully is not your friend. Why would you want a friend that treats you like dirt, anyway? Next time, take a stand and be yourself. It's time to make a change!

3. Growl Girrrl

Okay, so you may have stopped the Bully at her game a time or two. You're definitely not afraid to stand up for yourself. You have so much power, and now you just have to learn how to use it, not abuse it. Your actions make you more and more like the Bully, instead of the special, strong-willed girl you really are. Imitating bad behavior isn't the way to solve problems, so don't get caught in that dangerous pattern. You have the power to make the Bully back down, so be smart and make a fresh start—no more bully behavior!

4. Real Girl Power

You're focused on your own agenda, and there's plenty to do without worrying about the Bully and her antics. Your life is an open road, and the Bully is like one of the bumps along your way—you just move around her and get on with your life. If you can't get her off of your back, you know what to do: tell her to stop it now, or you'll find a way to stop it yourself. You're on the right track, so just continue to let your girl power shine! Don't let anyone get in your way.

Even though more and more teachers and adults are realizing the problems that the Bully and her crew can cause, it's definitely not something that will go away overnight. In fact, the bully problem is still spreading, even as you read this.

> At our middle school, girls who smile and enjoy school get picked on. People say things like they have a "Kool-Aid" smile and that they are weird, and then they shove them "accidentally." Yeah, right. These kinds of mean comments and all that pushing and shoving can really lower a girl's self-esteem and make her hate school. ~Janeen, 13

And what starts in middle school usually continues into high school, where what was just an instance of a little shoving here and there can escalate to scary proportions. It can even turn the girls who were bullied into real mean chicks.

> What's the big deal? You don't need to bring an AK-47 or some C-14 to school and kill somebody. Jeez! Go get a "101 Ways to Make Other Girls Feel Miserable" book. If you kill the bullies, then you're not able to tell your tormenters how bad you got them back. ~ Gwyn, 18

Without solutions for girls who are the victims of bullying, a vicious cycle starts. Things go from bad to worse quickly. And that's so unfair! You and your group of friends need an environment that's totally safe and geared to your success.

So how can you stop the mean chicks and negative cliques, and nix their dirty tricks?

Bully Smarts: What Should You Know about the Bully?

Arm yourself with the following info on the Bully:

* Even though the Bully causes problems for you, *you* aren't the cause of *her* problems. By understanding this, you empower yourself to start on a path of positive change that will continue for years to come.
* Most bullies come from an environment where they were bullied or abused themselves; when they bully you, they're imitating the way they were raised. This is too bad, but it's still no excuse. After all, many girls have issues around their home life and yet they don't take it out on others.
* Bullies may feel insecure or unloved, and have little or no confidence. Often their self-esteem is very low. By bullying you, they're trying to make themselves feel better, but that's not going to work. You're not their punching bag!

Rapid Response: What You Should Do about the Bully

When faced with the Bully head on, try one of these options:

1. While it won't work forever, avoiding the Bully as much as possible is one option until you've figured out exactly what to do.

2. Next, change your attitude toward the Bully. You can handle her better than you think! You can start by going to school each day strong and prepared, instead of scared and intimidated. Have a bully-proof comment ready, such as "I'm sorry you're having a bad day!" Then step around her and carry on as usual.

3. Stand up for yourself! If the Bully is bothering you, tell her to cut it out. If the bullying continues, say, "I told you to stop it or else." If she says, "Or what?" Say, "That's for me to know and you to find out." Many bullies are basically cowards. Once she sees that you're taking a stand, she'll probably back down.

First Person: What I Went Through—A Real Life Story

During my childhood, I was a very self-conscious person. I was often criticized for my appearance. I had a small number of friends and associates. In seventh grade, there was a group of girls that thought they were bad. They walked around acting like no one could ever step in their way at any time, like they could get any boy whenever they wanted. I was a girl they hated because I wasn't as pretty or the same size as them. I was overweight and wore glasses, and when I passed them, they hit me every time. They slapped me, and punched me, and pushed me down the stairs like I was nothing.

One of the girls in this group was once my friend in a lower grade. She had made up her mind that I was unfit to be her friend, so she stopped talking to me. Another girl in the group was my cousin, and we didn't talk because she didn't like me. And the other girls were project chicks.

Not much later, there was a talent show coming up. So me and my friends tried to figure out what our performance would be.

I decided to sing, with my friends doing the backup, and the group of mean chicks came up with a dance.

Finally, it was time for the big rehearsal. I made it through, but the group of girls didn't make the cut. After two practices it was time for the real talent show. My friends wore a cute combination of Hispanic clothes that were all the same. I wore a dark green dress with dark green heels, white pearls, and a shawl wrapped around my arms. I also wore a little bit of makeup. I sang my heart out that night and all of my family was there.

Even the group of mean girls was there, jealous because I made it into the talent show. They made faces and laughed while I sang, but I ignored them. When I was finished, I got a standing ovation, so I bowed and then left the stage. My mother was in tears and I was sooo happy. After that it was time for the judges to announce the winner.

Third place was given to one of my friends. Second place went to a girl who was a ballerina. When it was time for first place, I felt chills go up my spine. And when they announced that the first place winner was me, I was thrilled. I ran and hugged my mom and family. Then I went to get my prize of $100.

The group of mean girls came up and tried to hold a conversation, but I just turned my back and hugged my friends. There was no need to say anything—I was a winner!

~LaRosa, 16

First Rate: Grade the Girls

A+ Because you were strong, LaRosa, in the face of all those mean chicks trying to pull you down. They treated you so badly, but you didn't let it get to you and destroy you. Instead, you clung to your dream and worked for it; you persevered. You were a winner even before you won the big talent show. Congratulations!

 Being constantly dissed by other girls when I was younger made me who I am today ~ an achiever.
~Caitlin, 17

Dear Diary

So now it's time to get real with yourself. Have you ever been treated meanly by other girls? Or have you seen one of your friends suffer because of other girls? When did it happen and what were the circumstances? Maybe someone forced you to give up your seat on the bus, or cut in front of you in line, or maybe even hit you or physically hurt you in some way. Surely, these things hurt you. But you probably couldn't express how much it hurt while you were in school. Well, now it's time to get those feelings out. Write down one of those instances and how it made you feel. Don't hold back! It's okay to cry, or feel angry, or both. That's what your journal is for.

Next, write down how you overcame that feeling. Did you fight back? Did you walk away? How do you feel about how you handled it? What exactly did you do?

And finally, make a list of other ways that you could have used to handle the situation. Was there something you could have done differently? Better? Keep these things in mind for next time. Make a second list, this time, as if you were writing it for younger girls who find themselves in the crosshairs of the Bully. What advice would you give them?

Remember, no one is judging you here. Your writing is all for you. By using your journal, you are revealing the real strength in you.

Fab Fixes for Whatever Attitude Ails You

Some days, let's face it, we all get up on the wrong side of the bed. We just don't feel like ourselves. We don't mean to, but we snarl and bark and sling things and fling words. Sure, on days like that, we may slam doors a little louder than usual. Or when we drop our books on our desks, we may do it with an extra *bang!*

Though our anger doesn't last forever, sometimes we're just mad because something doesn't go our way. It might be some dumb little thing or bigger stuff that ticks us off. Oh, you know: You get a zit when you're trying to look your best. Or you get your period at exactly the wrong moment. Or you have that substitute teacher who's always calling on you the moment you don't know something. It's easy to take our anger out on others when we're feeling this way. Maybe it's *too* easy!

 I get picked on a lot. Like when our teacher is going over something and calls on you. If you don't know the right answer, all the girls will laugh. ⌒ Jessica, 14

And suddenly all the little mean things other girls have done to us get on our nerves and get blown way out of proportion. We feel like the world doesn't like us, and we want to get everybody back, starting with our little brother, our older sister, or maybe even our best friends. What we feel like is lashing out or punching something or someone, or kicking something or someone. Why is everything going wrong today?

So how can you handle it? What can you do on days when you have a real bad attitude or a real Mad-itude?

Rx—Mastering Mad-itude

Do 3x a day:

1. Say as little as possible, because you know once you open your little trap, you're more likely to snap, and that's not cool.
2. Give people around you a fair warning. From parents to teacher to your best buds, it's better to let them know your 'tude isn't what it should be. Say, "I'm having a bad day, okay? So, can we discuss this tomorrow? Please?"
3. Then as soon as you get home from school, go for the comfort. You know what makes you feel better, don't you? It's that soft cuddly top you love, no matter that it won't win any fashion awards. So put it on, play your fave CD, and unwind for a bit. Later, if that Mad-itude has begun to fade, maybe make that quick dash into your favorite store and do some browsing—maybe even buy something new.

Try to have something fun planned. The madder you get, the radder your plans should be, after first getting your mom's permission, of course. So make something that rocks happen to you on a mad day. Then in no time your Mad-itude will turn into Glad-itude. You'll stop pouting and spouting off.

You're in charge of your life, your happiness, and your moods! While sometimes we can't help but brood, just make sure it doesn't last.

The Bottom Line

Here's what you need to remember about bullies:

★ There are lots of bullies in school and in your neighborhood. They're up to no good, but now you can deal with them because now you know what drives them. You understand that their actions don't have to do with you, but with their own problems.

★ It's okay to feel sorry for the Bully and the things she's had to endure, but that shouldn't be your main goal. Your main goal is to empower yourself and, through that, start a trend that stops the bullying.

★ Be strong, devise a plan of action, and see it through. First, tell the Bully to stop—loud and clear. If she doesn't stop, take action. Get your friends together, stand up to the Bully, and let her know you are not afraid. Finally, if the bullying persists and you really need a solution, report it to a trusted teacher.

Chapter 5

"The Traitor"

Words to Live By: As long as you don't forgive, who and whatever it is will occupy a rent-free space in your mind. ~Isabelle Holland

What Makes a Girl a Traitor?

Let's face it, there's nothing worse than getting betrayed by your friend. One minute she's your best bud, and the next she's dumped you for a new group of friends and acting like you don't exist. Or maybe she's flirting with your boyfriend. Or even worse, maybe she blabbed something about you that was supposed to be top secret. You thought you could trust her, but you're realizing now that you can't. You've just encountered . . . "the Traitor."

 Having your best friends treat you mean can really mess with your self-esteem. ~ Carole, 14

Dear Dr. Erika:

Nicole was always the flirtatious type. She was short, super skinny at 95 pounds, and yet had an ego that surpassed her small size. Getting all the attention in the room was her one goal, and I discovered to what great lengths she would go to get it.

She had been one of my very best friends for three years—we ran track together—when I told her I was interested in a shy boy, Chad, who indicated that he liked me as well.

So right away Nicole and I organized a group date with Chad, Nicole, Ann, me, and several other good friends. But I could tell it was tearing Nicole up to see Chad giving me all his attention and not her.

A true friend is supposed to be happy for you when you find a good guy to date, but not Nicole. She began flirting with him before my very eyes. It was outrageous.

I am a shy person as is Chad, so Nicole set out to prove she could be wilder and more outgoing than I am. I never had any classes with Chad, but when I would be walking down the hall with Nicole and my other friends and we'd pass him, Nicole's voice was always the loudest when saying hello. Hi Chad! Hi Chad!!!

When Chad and I started drifting apart, it took me a while to realize that Nicole was the cause. It all sunk in a few months later when Chad asked Nicole to the prom and not me. She would not even tell me herself that Chad had asked her because she knew it would upset me so. After the prom Nicole said Chad was a real bore, and that she didn't even like him, so why did she have to ruin things for me?

And that's not all. Nicole made it a point of excluding me. When there was a party going on, she would always keep it a secret from me. I found that out when Penny, another friend of mine, asked me if I was going to the class cookout. I told her I didn't know what she was talking about and she said she'd told Nicole several times to inform me.

Another time was when my mom decided to drive Nicole and me home from the mall. Nicole's cell phone rang. It was one of her multitude of conquests who asked her if she wanted to go bowling. Nicole had the nerve to ask my mom to drop her off at the bowling alley and didn't even ask me if I wanted to come along.

Wonder what acts of inconsideration and carelessness she'll pull next?

~Shelby, 16

Dear Dr. Erika:

All year long, my friend Janet has been talking about the big party her parents will give her when she turns sixteen. It's going to be a huge, huge event with lots of kids invited, including boys! And not just from our school, but from some of the other schools as well. And some will even come from out of town. Janet's family is from all over; she even has cousins in England. Anyway, like every day we've been talking about it. I've helped her with most of the planning because Janet doesn't have the most creative ideas. She's so smart but I always help her with something out of the ordinary, something way out. So here we've been putting our heads together and making all the great plans—I spent hours coming up with songs she likes, there's going to be a deejay! And decorating ideas, stuff to go on the tables. There's going to be a tent and a cookout and we made a list of games together. I even helped write out the invitations.

Day before yesterday all the girls at school—way most of them—well, quite a few were showing off their invitations. It made me so happy. This was MY work! When they said, "Did you get yours?" I had a sinking feeling but said, "Oh, the mail's slow at our house," but the invitation didn't come. And when I mentioned it to Janet, like maybe it got lost, she turned pink all over and said her mother said the guest list was way long and she had to cut it and you know . . .

When I heard her go on and on, I felt like MY heart broke all to pieces like when somebody drops a Chinese Ming vase!

~Lynda, 17

FYI

A traitor is someone who betrays a sacred trust. In your life that means this is a girl who's close to you and has been for some time and still she betrays you. She misleads and deceives you, and not just in minor stuff, but in some major way. So being the victim of a traitor can really hurt.

 The worst I ever felt was when it came out that my 4-ever best friend told everybody what she promised never to tell anybody. ~ Mikki, 15

A traitor is sneaky; a traitor is dishonest. She's so two-faced that she plays her part perfectly, and you never suspect anything. Why would you? After all this girl is an insider, goes to most of your classes, is in your clubs, even lives in your neighborhood and plays on the softball team with you.

Sure. You've known her like forever, and she's actually your best friend or like a close sister. She's your sole and soul *confidant*. She's someone you feel like you can tell *anything* to and you know she'll keep quiet about it. She would never, ever tell; that's what she's promised you lots of times. And all this has been going on for years. And wow! You're just so glad you have her to confide in and goof around with. Whew, the things you two can get into.

Meanwhile, she's also sharing with you what's going on with her and talking frankly and holding nothing back. Maybe she's the one friend you rely on most. When something hits the fan, you can turn to her and just let it all out—whatever deep dark secrets you may harbor, or whatever not so great ideas or even great ones you have, even whatever it is you're ashamed of, even the things you have never, ever even admitted to yourself.

So yes, your friendship, your bond is sacred, at least to you. That's what makes the Traitor with her tricks one of the worst of the mean chick types—she's not as easy to spot as some of the others.

Then one day you find out that everything you have revealed in confidence gets blabbed about everywhere. This is a hard thing to take. It feels like your feelings have been trashed!

 When your best friend turns on you and says mean things to you—or about you—oh, the pain and agony! You can't really put it in words. ～ Phoebe, 15

What a horrible wake-up call this is, to find out that who you thought was your best pal is really *against* you and never was truly for you to begin with. That kind of realization can really hurt you deeply.

Universal High School

Lainie and Tonya have known each other all their lives and now attend the same high school. And yet suddenly something went wrong between them. Here's their story, according to Tonya:

Lainie's always been my *best* friend among all my friends and we've trusted each other completely. I've told her things I've never told anyone else: things that bother me, embarrassing stuff, like how my chin looks *lopsided*.

One day Lainie began talking about this new guy she liked. I didn't even know who he was and figured Lainie and he wouldn't last very long because Lainie's "relationships" never did.

When I finally met the new guy, needless to say I was not impressed. He was the opposite of what she had always looked for in a boyfriend, and I wasn't the only one who didn't like him. None of our other friends did, but we all tried to be nice for her sake, which wasn't easy.

He seemed jealous of my relationship with Lainie, and due to this, he was always making jabs at me. I got used to it, but it still hurt especially when I realized that Lainie ignored my pain. Her making excuses or ignoring his digs at me was agonizing and at times almost brought me to tears. Then everything really hit the fan.

While I spent the night at her house, Lainie called the guy at midnight to talk. I got bored and fell asleep. When my mom asked me later about the night, I said, not thinking, "I fell asleep while Lainie was still talking on the phone."

That simple statement caused all sorts of trouble. My mother repeated it to Lainie's parents, who were suspicious of the new guy to begin with, and they ran with what I had said.

The next day at school Lainie confronted me. I told her I was innocent because I had never told anyone she was talking to her boyfriend at midnight. And I was very disappointed that she didn't have enough faith in me to believe that I would *never* tell anyone about her talking to him so late.

To avoid making her even madder, I decided to keep my distance from Lainie for a while. Instead of realizing that I was trying to give her time to cool down, she saw this as proof of my guilt.

There were several more confrontations: Lainie wouldn't give because she believed it was my fault; I wouldn't give because I felt I was innocent in the whole matter. But what was the worst, Lainie told her side to everyone in our group, so they *all* turned against me. I'd done nothing and yet they acted as if it was my fault. Even worse, she blabbed about *my* secrets. I know because even completely strange girls started staring at me and whispering about my "chin thing." This upset me so much I could hardly keep going, and it lasted until the school year was over. By then Lainie's relationship with the new guy was way ancient history. Now we're good friends again, sorta anyway. However, to this day, I can't get over the fact that Lainie ever thought I'd *betrayed* her. She betrayed me!

<FAST QUIZ>

Traitors Among Us—Beware!

So you see how sometimes even the best of friends can suddenly start acting like traitors, so you've got to guard yourself against this type of behavior! Here's a way to find out if you're vulnerable to the kind of betrayal we're talking about. Just take this little quiz:

1. You have been assigned a major project that requires interviewing older people in your neighborhood and asking them about World War II. You and your best bud spend hours formulating your questions and discussing how you will record the answers and how to videotape the participants. You're so psyched about this assignment, which will be *the* major grade for this semester. When you're ready to start, your best friend says she's decided to work with another girl. You:

   a. Hide your hurt feelings and tell her it's okay. But what if she steals your ideas and gets a better grade than you? Oh, well. There's nothing you can do about it now. Besides, you've never been one to stand out in the crowd.
   b. Drop your project entirely and ask if you can join in their group. You let them use all of your ideas and research and add it to their own, even though they don't seem very appreciative. It's better than working by yourself, and besides, there's not as much work to do with three of you splitting the responsibilities.

c. You're really ticked off that she bailed on you, but you fight fire with fire. You add up all the hours you already put into this project and tell your "best" friend she better give you major credit in her report, or she can't use the information at all. Plus, you make sure to spread it around your group of friends that she totally ditched you. If you get them all on your side, then she'll feel extra guilty about skipping out. Two can play at this game!

d. You pair up with another girl who doesn't have a partner and do the best work ever in your life. But you're hurt, and that's normal. Once you've had the chance to stop steaming at her, write her a note or give her a call after school and tell her how you feel. If she's a true friend, she'll listen and understand, and maybe the two of you can work it out. If she gets angry or defensive, maybe it's time to realize that your best bud doesn't have the best intentions.

2. You're trying out for the Junior Follies—the annual student talent show at your school. For weeks, you and your best friend have been rehearsing a routine for your fave song. The plan is that you will sing and your best friend will dance. She's been taking ballet lessons for eons. But on the day of dress rehearsal, your friend totally changes her tune and decides she wants to dance alone to a recorded version of the song. You:

a. Drop out of the show. What's the use—it will be sooo embarrassing when two different acts use the same song. And there's no way you can get up on that stage all by yourself! Besides, she's a better dancer than you are a singer, anyway. Why not let her have the spotlight?

b. Beg and plead for her to stay with you for the act. You promise her you'll buy her tickets to the next Matt Damon flick, let her borrow that fave sweater that you *never* let her lay a hand on—you even promise that you'll go out on that blind date with her cousin (which you've been avoiding). If that fails, you tell on her to the faculty sponsor and *make* her perform with you. Whatever it takes for her to get up there and do a little pas de bourrée or pirouette—anything to avoid being on that stage alone in front of the whole school!

c. Cause a scene that would make even the snottiest prima donna shake in her shoes. You remind her that she wouldn't even *have* a routine without you since the whole thing was your idea in the first place! You stomp around, tell everyone what a traitor she is, and scream until you're hoarse. That way you'll lose your singing voice and you can lay double blame on her skinny a _ _ when you have to quit the show.

d. Take a little time to get over the shock, then recoup and regroup. Maybe it's better this way. You know you'll give it your best shot; you'll just get out there and sing like Celine Dion at her last concert. Who knows, there may even be a couple of record company scouts in the audience. Hey, you could end up on the next *American Idol!*

3. It's prom time, you and your best friend are totally dateless. The guys you're interested in all have girlfriends, and the dudes who're interested in you are duds. No prob—you decide that you'll go by yourselves and have a blast anyway. You'll be the divas of the dance with your awesome 'do's and sexy shoes. And you won't have to worry about impressing some dumb guy. One hour before the prom, your friend calls to tell you she has a date! With Clyde, the most pitiful drooling little perv in the whole school. Nobody likes him, not because of his looks or nerd quotient, but because he carries porn pix around and always tries to look down girls' shirts! You:

a. Stay in your room with a pint of cookie dough ice cream and a DVD of *Pretty Woman*. A dynamic duo would have been totally cool, but you can't believe you got dumped for Creepy Clyde. It would be too embarrassing to show up all alone. Better luck next year!

b. Rush excitedly over to your friend's house, help fix her hair and makeup, and make sure to bring your dress with you. With any luck, she can fix you up with Creepy Clyde's buddy, Loony Luther. Hey, it may not be your dream date, but it's better than staying home.

c. Call Clyde and tell him every nasty thing your friend has ever said about him, every last detail! You even manage to come up with a few more of your own, and you're quite proud of your creativity. You warn him to stay away from your friend, or you'll turn him in for carrying around porno mags. If you're dateless for the prom, you'll make sure your friend will be, too!

d. Go to the prom dressed to kill, boogie down all night long, and have a blast. Your friend is on her own trip, but you don't need a guy to have fun. These days, flying solo is just as hip as doing the date thing. Meanwhile, you spot your bud in the corner, trying to keep Clyde from breathing down her neck. You'll give her a call later to get the dish and comfort her—but you're not going to let her decision bring you down.

4. A special guy you've admired from way back sends you an e-mail that's sweet and touching. It's all about how he's been noticing you, too, and wants to talk to you tomorrow after second period. You're freaking out with joy and forward this e-mail to your best friend, making sure to label it TOP SECRET!!!! Your hopes for romance are crushed when you discover, to your horror, that she's forwarded it to the whole class! You:

a. Feel like dropping out of school. You'd rather die than face your crush, and you definitely can't face your classmates tomorrow. But maybe if you're late to first period and have your mom check you out early, you can ignore them and they'll forget about it. As far as your "ex" best friend goes, you're too hurt to face her, so you just lay low until the whole thing blows over.

b. See your friend in the hallway and pretend as though nothing has happened. After all, if you're ticked off at her, you won't have anyone to sit with at lunch or to hang out with this weekend. So she made a mistake. When you see your crush in the hall, you avoid his gaze and act like you don't even know him. It's better than dealing with the humiliation of having your feelings exposed. There are plenty of other fish in the sea, right?

c. Immediately design a wild Web page, detailing all of your friend's deepest and most personal issues. You're not planning on being a Web designer for nothing! The page features everything and anything you can dish about your friend—the first guy she kissed, every tiny move her boyfriend ever made on her, whatever will make her curl up with mortification. As the coup de grace, you post that awful picture of her that you swore you'd never show to anyone, the one you took just after she had her wisdom teeth out and her face was totally swollen. Then you forward the link to everyone in your class. You are a girl of the cyber world, and you fight fire with fire!

d. Are totally embarrassed—and furious. And it's your total right to be. After you've cooled down a little, you have a long talk with your friend. You tell her how much she's hurt you and that she's broken your trust. You also let her know that you won't put up with this type of thing very long before you tell her to hit the road. As for your crush—well, it's not exactly a great storybook romance, but since he knows how you feel anyway, you might as well act on it. You never know where it could lead!

Answers

Now it's time to find out how you did. Total up your answers.

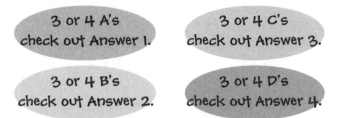

3 or 4 A's
check out Answer 1.

3 or 4 C's
check out Answer 3.

3 or 4 B's
check out Answer 2.

3 or 4 D's
check out Answer 4.

If you have a mixture of A's, B's, C's, and D's, look at all the answers. Obviously, there's a little bit of everything in you, which is great. Now can you work on getting a little more of that Answer # 4 attitude?

1. Too Timid!

Pick your head up, girl! Haven't you learned by now that running away from your problems will never solve them? Next time, just deal with it. Let the Traitor know that she hurt you and that you're not going to put up with it. If telling her face to face isn't your thing, maybe you can write her a note and let her know how you feel. If you want to make good friends, you've got to be a good friend, and part of being a good friend is being able to talk about how you feel. If you don't take a stand for yourself, your friends are going to keep walking all over you. Don't be discouraged, though. Knowledge is power. So take the power you get from this book and hold your head up high!

2. Hanging with the Enemy

Why do you keep clinging to this friend when she treats you like an enemy? You owe yourself more than hanging around with a dishonest friend and making yourself miserable. You deserve better than that, and there are plenty of girls to hang around with. You're a cool chick, not a doormat. Try giving some other girls a chance and see what it's like to have real friends, not passing trends!

3. Jungle Jane

What are you trying to gain from getting back at your formerly "best" friend? What's done is done, so turning into a mean queen yourself isn't going to help a bit. Sure, she broke your trust, and that really hurts. Standing up for yourself is definitely a plus, but waging a war of revenge isn't the way to win. That only makes you a loser in the end. You're strong and sweet, and you want to stay that way. Playing these games will only make you sour.

4. Traitor Triumph

What a girl! You let yourself feel the pain that always comes when someone you care about betrays you. And you face up to the Traitor! But then you don't wallow in your misery for long because you know there are so many great chicks out there, and it won't be long until you will find one that's a true friend, not a jealous weasel. So forge new friendships—with both girls and guys. The world is your oyster. It's up to you to find the pearls.

Traitor Smarts—What Should You Know about the Traitor?

A one-time occurrence of betrayal can be bad enough, but what if you just found out that your best bud has been betraying you for months? What you need to know:

★ The Traitor has most likely been betrayed herself in the past, but rather than learn from this bad experience and become an especially good friend, she has become an imitator of treacherous behavior.

★ She doesn't know the true meaning of friendship. Therefore, the Traitor breaks a trust as easily as she'd snap a twig. If you still hang out with her, proceed with extreme caution!

★ Whatever problems she's had in the past, don't excuse the Traitor's behavior. Once she's betrayed you, stay away from her for as long as you wish. Maybe slowly and over time, trust can be rebuilt, but don't feel any pressure. Think about the Traitor long and hard, and then *you* decide if you want to give her another chance.

Rapid Response: What You Should Do about the Traitor

Want some top tips when faced with the Traitor?

1. Know that traitors don't come with a warning sign. No matter what you may think at the time, you can and will get over being hurt by a friend. It may take a while, but everything worthwhile does, and rebuilding trust after you've cleared the air isn't easy. But it will benefit you. You'll emerge from this stronger and better. And you may even be able to teach the Traitor how great a *real* friend can be!

 Disappointment is something that we as human beings must learn to accept. My disappointment came in the form of a dear longtime friend and confidant who did me wrong. ⁓ Pam, 16

2. Whatever you do, don't get cynical and turn your back on other girls forever. There are real friends out there, who will be loyal to you no matter what. Don't start doubting that there can be real friends, like Allie did after her longtime best friend suddenly revealed her true colors.

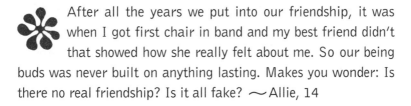 After all the years we put into our friendship, it was when I got first chair in band and my best friend didn't that showed how she really felt about me. So our being buds was never built on anything lasting. Makes you wonder: Is there no real friendship? Is it all fake? ⁓ Allie, 14

Real friendships take years to build, and it's up to you to use good judgment in choosing your friends. But time alone isn't the only way to measure the strength of a friendship.

 Face it: Time doesn't determine how good a friendship is; it's the trust and other things that go along w/it. ⁓ Mary, 17

First Person: What I Went Through—A Real Life Story

Leigh and I have been friends for a long, long time. We live in the same neighborhood and officially met at the beginning of middle school. Ever since, we started the tradition to always go holiday shopping together at the mall. We picked the first Saturday in December as *the day* and discussed it all year long. Many of our other friends would join us whenever they could, but the two of us *never* missed our yearly routine.

It would always be exactly the same: First, we walked to the center where the little kids had their picture taken with good ol' Santa Claus (ho-ho-ho!) sitting on a bench in front of a giant gingerbread house. We'd spend half an hour watching them and laughing over the cute kids and reminiscing about the time when we were little kids ourselves. Then we'd amble over to the food court for lunch. It was always veggie pizza and chocolate ice cream with sprinkles. And then, lists in hand, we'd hit the stores hard and spend all our carefully saved cash.

This year, our senior year, Leigh changed schools. At first that was okay, but then we started not to talk and spend as much time together anymore. We used to talk and see each other every day, but now we were lucky if we did this three times a week.

Anyway, December was coming up. I'd been hoarding all the extra money I made baby-sitting, and I knew Leigh was doing exactly the same. This year, for the first time we'd really spend money like mad. Plus, the newspaper announced that several new stores would open—the kinds we really just love and had always talked about longingly!

Excitedly, I called Leigh a week before *the day* and asked her if she was planning to drive or should I. Well, did I get a surprise. Leigh said she was going on a family trip and would be out of town. Sorry.

I was astonished because that had never ever happened before, but I understood. I decided to go to the mall anyway with several other girls because the routine had become so drilled into my head. I guess the same thing had happened to Leigh, because when I got to the gingerbread house, there she was laughing and talking with some new friends.

It turned out she had lied to me: There was no family trip planned. But why couldn't she just have told me the truth? Now we still talk, we're still friends, but it's always like there's a cloud hanging over us.

~*Buffy, 18*

First Rate: Grade the Girls

C- Sure, Buffy feels betrayed, but that's because she's never cleared the air. The cloud of Leigh's lie is still hanging over their friendship.

But if Buffy wants to keep Leigh as a lifelong friend and wants to reclaim the real close friendship they used to have, some house-cleaning is called for. That should start with a heart-to-heart talk.

 It's good to always be open to meeting new people and having a variety of friends. Never depend on one person so, so much, okay? ~Alana, 17

 Always try to have more than one friend. If something was to happen in one relationship, it's important that a girl has other pals to turn to. So don't ever shut yourself off. No girl is an island, you know. ~Tangela, 16

Dear Diary

Have you ever been betrayed or turned on by a best friend? Was it someone you trusted with your deepest secrets? Whom you loaned money to and shared your lunch with and even loaned that cute new top to even though you hadn't even worn it yet?

If you have, write about it in your diary. Be sure to put in every thought that crossed your mind, every reaction, every feeling you had or still have. How did it make you feel to realize that your "friend" was just using you? Don't worry about how it sounds or if it doesn't make any sense; just get in out. Maybe you're better at poetry. If so, then write a poem. Whatever helps you get through your feelings, write it out—fuss and cuss as much as you want. This is no one's business but your own.

Next, make a list of all of the words that describe what our friend did, like: *lie*, *cheat*, *sneak*, etc. Look at the list closely. Next to each negative word, write down a positive word that turns things around. Look at this list even more closely, and make a promise to yourself that you'll put it to good use. These words are the way you'll treat all of your friends from now on.

Finding loyal true friends that last can be way tough. But don't give up. One of my supposed best friends was always plotting behind the scenes to keep me from making new friends. She wanted me to have <u>nobody</u>. But once I found out the truth, I felt sorry for her and was able to move on.
∼ Patty Ann, 17

Fab Fixes for Whatever Attitude Ails You

Growing up is a time of ups and downs and can be a roller coaster of emotions. One moment you're on top of the world; the next you feel lower than low. Remember, it's so normal to have fleeting feelings of inferiority. Also, sometimes you'll find yourself having negative feelings about other girls, too, even those who have never been mean to you. Suddenly, you're envious of some of them or wish they wouldn't win the tennis match, the swim team competition, or first place at the science fair.

But that's all part of growing into the wonderful person you're meant to be. Feeling conflicting emotions about yourself and your best pals is normal. Even the fact that you cover up any spiteful thoughts and congratulate your friends insincerely is normal, too.

You see, your emotional well-being is just growing along with the rest of you, and growth isn't always smooth and straightforward. There are a few detours ahead for everyone. Still, should you come down with a serious case of Fraud-itude, when suddenly you find yourself feeling jealous of your best friends and wishing bad things on them, and yet you act fakey nice, try using some of the tips below.

Rx—Fighting Fraud-itude
Do 1x a day every day:

1. Dismiss any unfriendly thoughts at once and replace them with positive, encouraging ones. For example, instead of thinking, "I want Cara to come in second," say out loud, "I hope Cara will get first place!" Fight the "green monster" of envy and you'll feel like you're on top of the world!

2. We all need an outlet for our mean or envious thoughts sometimes, but that doesn't mean we should take them out on our friends. Write them down in your diary instead to get them out of your system. Then forget about them. You'll see—just writing them down often erases them from your mind.

3. If a friend of yours points out that recently you've been acting like a witch, don't get all huffy. Take this as an opportunity to improve your character. Your friend wouldn't point out this flaw in you if she didn't care. Similarly, if it's you who's been treated treacherously, be as forgiving as you can. Try to give a real good friend another chance, but only if you feel you can. When dealing with traitors, your gut instinct will always be your best guide.

The Bottom Line
So, here's the bottom line on traitors:

★ The girl world can be tough, but remember, there are all kinds of great chicks out there just waiting to be your friends. Be resilient! By learning to bounce back from a bad situation or a betrayal, you're empowering yourself.

★ On the road to success (or maybe to graduation), try to think of betrayal as a lesson to be learned, not a permanent scar that you must carry with you. Life will be full of stumbling blocks. It's up to you whether you want to avoid them or overcome them. It's great to have friends that you trust, but beware of confiding too early on in a friendship. Take it easy, take it slow. Good friendships take a while to grow!

★ Know that friends can make mistakes, no matter how close you may be. Okay, so maybe your friend acted like a total rat. But deep down, if you know she's a great chick, full of fun times and great laughs and long talks, consider giving her another chance. To find out if your friendship is worth saving, have a serious talk with the Traitor. If she apologizes and says she's really sorry, that's a good sign. After a long talk and some fence mending, your friendship could become stronger than before.

Part II
The "In" Crowd

Now you know the five basic types of mean chicks and how to deal with them. But what happens when several of them get together? When girls gang up on one of their classmates, it automatically makes them feel more powerful and often they abuse that power.

So of course, you wonder: Is there *anything* you can do to protect yourself should a group of girls target you? Of course! And one of the most important things to do is be in the know. Knowing who you are and where you stand is the best way to arm yourself. Popularity, like so many things in life, may come and go. But being aware of who you are and what you want (and choosing good friends along the way)—will stay with you no matter what!

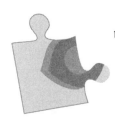 Many words have been said about my looks, but I have some great friends who take up for me. By them being there, it makes me feel better. ∼Becca, 16

Yes, friends really count. They can talk you through your many disappointments, heal a broken heart, or even make you feel better about that zit that came out of nowhere!

As I got older, I hoped my looks would start changing. See, "the Nose" runs in my family, but my friends always help me laugh it off. Works every time. ∽ Lynne, 17

In the following pages, you'll start to understand what happens when girls interact in a group or clique. You'll learn all about clique behavior and how to handle it. So, let's get started by talking about what happens deep within a group of girls, specifically, what makes a clique tick?

Chapter 6

Just One of the Girls

So let's look at girls in groups more closely. What makes them act the way they do in packs? Starting with the animal world, scientists long ago decided to call the most aggressive or leading animal in a given group, the *alpha* of the breed. Take a pack of wolves, for example. The *alpha* wolves run the show, whereas the *beta* wolves are the less aggressive wolves that are vying for the position of *alpha*. Once this was identified in different animal families, it was only a small jump to identify a similar trait in men, which resulted in the term *alpha males*. Even more recently, researchers have begun applying the term to girls as well. Why?

Because the first letter in the Greek alphabet, *alpha*, is translated in English as the letter A and also as "first in any group." So when you identify different types of girls, why shouldn't you begin with Type A, the alpha girl?

And beta, the second letter in the Greek alphabet, is translated in English as a B or as "the second or runner-up in any group."

So it makes sense to call some girls *alphas* and other girls *betas*. In the English language, we'd call them the "A girls" (Admired by a lot of girls) and the "B girls" (Busy bees, who would love to be A's, if only they could).

But there is another type of girl, a girl who is independent-minded, a girl who is comfortable in her originality and who is not interested in alpha or beta status. This type of girl cares about those around her and is interested in growing, learning, and finding her place in society with smarts and style. You may have read about her in the news or on the Net—she is the *gamma* girl. Because you picked up this book, because you know all about the stuff that goes on in the girl world, and because you want to change it, *you* are a gamma girl, too. As a gamma girl, you are making contributions to the world around you, maybe without even knowing it, because of the example you set for others. Here are a few of your gamma girl contributions:

- ★ Understanding the girl behavior around you.
- ★ Setting an example of how to act for younger girls.
- ★ Showing the alphas and betas how to become better, kinder, and more caring girls through your own behavior.

These contributions make you a great addition to any group. Still, you may see a little alpha or beta in yourself from time to time, and that's fine. It's all part of what we call *group dynamics*.

Dear Dr. Erika:

Last week I was interviewed for the local newspaper paper. What happened was, there was this big incident of cheating at our school. One of the girls went in the teachers' lounge after school and just "happened" to find the key to their trig unit test. So what she did was copy it and pass it around. I'm not in this class but heard all about it. Anyway, this reporter lady corners my friend and me before school to get our opinion—and I was speechless. Not! I just didn't know what to say. Some of the "cheaters" are my friends, so I didn't want to condemn them in public. But yet what they did was wrong! Still and all, I waited for the girls I was with to voice their opinions, and then I mumbled something way lame. But this was MY one chance to speak up—and I blew it.

~Meredith, 16

Dear Dr. Erika:

Whenever there's a big project being talked about in school, like a fundraiser for the homeless or a toy drive for kids in Afghanistan, our homeroom teacher always asks for a volunteer to head it up.

You see, we're all juniors and you know how slack seniors can get. Our teachers call it "senioritis," so we juniors have to do most of the projects.

Anyway, when MY teacher calls for volunteers I never raise MY hand. Reason is, I kind of want to do it but I don't know if I can. Then this other girl is like, "I'll do it," and it never fails. Our homeroom turns in the fewest number of cans or cash, whatever. But we never win.

I always know I could do it better, getting the other students to contribute and so on, but still I always hesitate.

~Twayna, 16

FYI

Group dynamics is defined as the "relationship between movable forces in a number of individuals aggregated together."

Excuse me?

Okay, in plain English it translates to this: Group dynamics deals with what people do when they're in a bunch. That's especially important for girls because they're rarely alone, at least not in school. Almost every class has twenty or more students. And some classes have over thirty-five enrollees. So, from the moment you enter kindergarten, you're accustomed to groups. Naturally, by the time you're your age, you're used to lots of girls being around. And sure, you don't want them all to be your friends. But it's no surprise that you'd want a particular group of girls to hang out with.

Group dynamics is fascinating because it deals with how girls like you act in a class or club: how you look at one another and subsequently behave. What part of your nature comes to the forefront most often when you're around your peers? Do you turn into a leader, a follower, or a team player?

For instance, being a team player means:

* ★ Doing what it takes to make the team triumph.
* ★ Being a leader sometimes.
* ★ Being a follower another time while showing respect and cooperating with other girls, teachers, and coaches so that everyone can benefit.

First Person: What I Went Through—A Real Life Story

When I was in eighth grade we had to put on a holiday pageant, the Festival of Lights, and I was asked to read a poem, but I messed up. I got so nervous I forgot all but the first line, which I repeated over and over. How embarrassing! I was praying that a trap door would open up and I could jump in and disappear.

That didn't happen, but as it turned out, my single-line poem wasn't that bad. At least I didn't just get up there and go, "um, um, um." Still, ever since I've gotten the reputation that I'm the person that's much better with the set and the props and begging everyone's mom to let us scour their attic for costumes.

But that's all I was asked to do from then on. It seemed like word of my set-designing talents was passed along from grade to grade. In each new grade level, the teacher asked me to do the behind-the-scenes stuff, even the lighting!

But this year, on the day of the performance the star got sick. There was an understudy but she hadn't really paid attention, so when the drama teacher called on her, she refused to go on. The teacher looked sick! So I said I would try. By then I knew the whole play backward and forward. So that evening, I stepped on stage. I made a few minor flubs, but you know what? The show went on—and later the teacher said it was really truly the best Festival of Lights ever. Because of me! Because I'm a shining light!

~ *Tammy, 17*

First Rate: Grade the Girls

A+ Tammy took charge of the situation. She knew what she wanted, and she went after it. And she succeeded! She went from the set designer to the star, and all because she had the courage to speak up. There's nothing wrong with being a set designer; nothing wrong with doing the lighting. Both are wonderful ways of expressing artistic talent. But let Tammy's story be a lesson: Nobody should limit your possibilities. Make up your own mind and shine. This is your time!

<FAST QUIZ>

Group Gauge—What Part of the Group Are You?

Have you ever wondered what your place is in a group? Take this quiz:

1. You and your friends have been assigned an oral presentation on Elizabethan drama. You all had tons of fun writing reports, making posters, even looking up the hottest fashions back then and researching the music and menus of that bygone era. Today it's time to give your presentation. You:

   a. Volunteer to hold up the posters, which are terrific to hide behind. You don't want the whole class to eagle eye you and catch sight of the bad 'do you're sporting today!

   b. Sashay around the room, passing out the little crumpets you stayed up all night baking. That way the other students will have something to focus on besides giving you the once-over like they would if you'd stand in front of the class. Anyway, a moving target gathers no cruel stares.

   c. Wear an Elizabethan costume with wig and makeup, read all seventy-two pages of your report (including footnotes!) out loud, daring any student to yawn. As the grand finale, you whip out a pop quiz and smile with delight at the moans and groans!

   d. Plan that each member of your group delivers a different part of the presentation. That way you all get a chance. Your Power Point presentation is stellar, and the class gets involved in a lively discussion after you've all finished your respective parts. You won't know your grade for a few days, but the bright smile from the teacher tells you there's nothing to worry about.

2. Your favorite teacher is out and there's a sub—a raw recruit, seems like. It's obvious that she doesn't know her lesson plan from her liver spots. After taking roll, the flustered older woman scribbles the assignments—*read pages 47 and 48 and do problems 1 to 15*—on the board, then sinks into the armchair behind the teacher's desk and pulls out a romance novel. Of course, the class goes nuts, talking and acting up. You:

   a. Move your desk to a corner, stuff Kleenex in your ears to drown out all of the chatter, pull out your latest Danielle Steel novel and find out what happened to jilted Jillian!

   b. Go up to the sub and get on her good side by telling her which students might cause trouble, so she better keep an eye on them.

   c. Jump up and yell, "Everybody, get your butts in your seats and shut up!" The late bell rings. Then you march to the front of the room, read page 47 out loud while the rest of the class yells back at you and pelts you with crumpled paper. You out-yell them while you duck. It's good exercise, but if those fools don't quit, you're going to turn them in to the principal.

   d. Make this suggestion to the sub after conferring with your friends, "Why don't we work in groups and divide up the problems?" Soon, the class quiets down as various clusters of kids start tackling their assignments. Afterward there's still time to chat, plus the lesson got done—sorta, anyway!

3. Volleyball practice has just begun when the coach is called to the main office for an important message, leaving you and your team members alone in the gym. Luckily, the first match is two weeks away. You:

a. Plop on the bleachers and nap, hoping the coach won't be back for a while. The warm-ups she makes you do are killers.

b. Look around to see what the rest of the girls are doing and try to blend in with the group that looks like they're having the most fun. It's better than just standing around.

c. Chase after the coach and get her whistle, then blow it as loud as you can. You never could resist being in charge! "Time for the drill," you tell the team. "Better hop to it . . . now run around the gym twenty-five times. Last one gets kicked off." That's not your decision to make, but you've got the whistle, so you're the boss!

d. Encourage the team to carry out practice as usual, starting with the warm-up. You do your stretches, then sprint up the bleachers, then a couple times around the gym. By the time the coach returns, you're in the midst of a good practice game—with almost no time wasted.

4. You stayed late after school to finish your watercolor painting for the spring art show. As you go to your locker before leaving the building, you notice a girl you don't know slumped on the floor by the water fountain. You:

a. Forget about your locker and scurry off. You don't want to get involved in whatever this is—some girl getting sick or ODing. Besides, if it's something illegal, you don't want to get into trouble.

b. Search the halls until you find someone else to go and check on her with you. There's safety in numbers, after all, and you don't want to be the only one involved!

c. Whip out your cell phone, call 911, and scream, "Get here on the double. There's been a school shooting! Well, maybe just a girl on drugs, or pregnant, or she fainted, or she was in a fight, well, maybe she turned her ankle. Who knows? Better not take any chances these days!"

d. Run over to the girl and ask what's wrong. It turns out this girl just has bad cramps. You help her to the nurse's office, make sure she gets some Midol, and ask if you can give her a lift home.

Answers

Now it's time to find out how you did. Total up your answers.

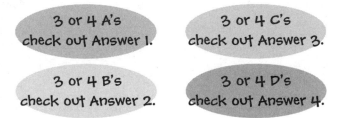

3 or 4 A's
check out Answer 1.

3 or 4 C's
check out Answer 3.

3 or 4 B's
check out Answer 2.

3 or 4 D's
check out Answer 4.

If you have a mixture of A's, B's, C's, and D's, look at all the answers. Obviously, there's a little bit of everything in you, which is great. Now can you work on getting a little more of that Answer #4 attitude?

1. Little Lamb Lost

You act like a little lamb lost most of the time, but why? What are you so scared of? School is your eminent domain, so go on, reign! You have the power to take action and deal with any problem that crops up. You just have to believe in yourself. Next time, try taking charge of a situation instead of blending in with the wallpaper. Part of group dynamics is actually being part of the group, after all. Even though it may not be your style, you should try speaking your mind once in a while. You'll be pleasantly surprised at the results.

2. Fear Factor

You're terrified to make a move without making sure you've got someone on your side, whether it's the substitute teacher or the fashionable clique. Instead of scrambling to join the herd, next time let your own voice be heard. It's time to start thinking for yourself and being proud of who you are. Do it now and find out how great it feels to seize the power that's in you.

3. Alpha . . . or Attitude?

You love to take charge, and that's great. But, remember, you're not the boss of others around you, so try to chill out just a little. Try taking a step back before you alienate everyone in your circle. Thinking for yourself is power, but thinking for others is abusing that power. So, just ease up and don't beat your friends over the head with a club when you want their cooperation. Don't yell at them, don't call them names, just tone down your Madame General act and learn to suggest, hint, and cooperate. Once you do this, you'll find your friends, classmates, and teammates much more willing to listen to your ideas.

4. Gamma Girl

Good job! Your independent spirit and caring nature will definitely help you thrive in the girl world. Keep up the gamma attitude and you'll definitely go far. You're a natural leader who doesn't need to force her way to the top. You're respected by your teammates and classmates, and you always follow the best course. In other words, you assess what's going on around you, while keeping your eyes on the prize. You let no one get in your way in practice, in performance, and in striving for perfection. Keep it up!

Group Dynamics Smarts—What Should You Know about Group Dynamics?

Now, putting it all together. Here's what you need to know:

* Group dynamics come into play everywhere girls are in groups. These groups may consist of girls you have things in common with—in your French III class, the art club, or the swim team. In those cases, the group can help you study more, learn new things about yourself, or set a new school record.
* But there are other groups that aren't so great. These groups have a different agenda from yours, and maybe you don't agree with them or get along with them very well. That's okay. You can't be best friends with everyone,

nor can you make everyone happy. Just do the best you can and be prepared to deal with all types of girls, no matter what group they come from.

No matter what kind of group you find yourself in, examine where you stand with them, then use your knowledge to your benefit. Go ahead. You want to be able to act, not react!

Rapid Response—What You Should Do about Group Dynamics

But how do you take the best actions and avoid negative reactions? Are you one of the girls or lost in the crowd? Try these steps:

1. First, don't let people dictate to you what part you should play in a group. Refuse to be pigeon-holed and assert yourself after giving yourself an inner checkup. Also know that in a group the team player approach is best, because it doesn't only zero in on one individual but on what's best for all of you. Foster team spirit, and then everyone wins.

2. Don't sit back every time and wait for other girls to make all the decisions. You know that you're a gamma, so take charge. Deep inside, you know you can do what needs to be done in each and every situation, and you have the power to make that happen.

3. There will be times when another girl might be best to head up a program or project. That's totally okay, too! The best part of being a gamma is being able to give support to those around you, and knowing your turn will come.

Fab Fixes for Whatever Attitude Ails You

Sometimes we all have major doubts about our talents. You know those days, don't you? It's a time when you begin to doubt that every little thing you ever did measured up. You worry that you're just not as good as other girls, no matter what. While we all have a bad day now and again, when you compare yourself with others and think only of your flaws, you fall into a bad trap. It's when you think the others have so much more in terms of IQ, talent, looks, everything—and you, you have only the leftovers! In short, what you have is a bad case of compar-atude. Instead of focusing on yourself and your fab future, you go around judging yourself against other girls in your group or class.

That happens to all of us at some time or another. As a result you just don't feel so cheerful. You mope and feel like you're at the end of your rope. Next thing, you're dragging, you're calling all homework busywork, and the teachers and coaches become slave drivers in your mind. And all because you're comparing yourself to others! Overall, all that contrasting yourself with other girls just makes you feel less peppy and maybe even less happy. So how can you change it?

RX—Conquering Compar-atude
Do 1x a day when you feel less than great:

1. Make a list of all of the things you do well—the things that make you uniquely, wonderfully YOU! Comparing yourself to others is useless and drains you. You're not *them*—those other girls you've been measuring yourself against. You're YOU, and that's the very best thing you can be.

2. Take a catnap when you come home from school or on weekend afternoons. It's good for your body, good for your soul, and a way to refresh yourself when you're feeling a little blue.

3. Be good to your body, and it will be good to you. Make sure you eat a good breakfast and maybe get a little exercise. Even a short walk outside can help to clear your head and get that compar-atude back in order. Do whatever you love that will help you recharge your battery and conquer a new day with the smarts and style you know you have.

The Bottom Line

Now that you know some things about group dynamics, here's the bottom line:

* Know where you stand in any group, and try your best to let your gamma qualities shine bright. You've got better things to do than get caught up in that alpha/beta competition.
* Be realistic about your abilities. Know when to be leader and when to be a strong member of the group. Always support those around you. This skill will help you to form strong relationships not only during your middle school and high school years, but also into college and beyond!
* So if you're the best person for the job—and you know if you are by your talents and your interests—then don't hold back. Roll up your sleeves and get busy; if there's something you want, go get it. You have the power to make your own happiness!

Chapter 7

The "Clique Chick"

Words to Live By: A diamond is a chunk of coal that made good under pressure. ~Anonymous

What Makes the "Clique Chick" Tick?

Watch out for this girl for she can be the most dangerous girl of all because she's a double or triple threat. She can be a snob, gossip, teaser, bully, traitor, or what have you. But her true colors come out only when she's surrounded by her group. When she's alone, she's not so bad, but when she's with her clique, it's a brand new ballgame. That's why some girls are more afraid of this type of girl than of any other.

> In today's society, girls tease other girls because they don't like who you are or because you're not in their clique. So they try to get you to be just like them and do things you shouldn't. But what can you do when the most popular girl expects you to do it? ~Josie, 15

You can do a lot to counteract the effects of those in a clique. Just because the most popular girl in school (and her gal pals) expect you to do something you know isn't right, you don't have to bite. So what's her deal, anyway? What's behind the Clique Chick? Let's find out.

Dear Dr. Erika:

One of the girls in my class gets everything—every award, every honor, every time she's the one nominated for whatever. It makes me sick. When there's a vote, I don't even participate anymore, because she gets it anyway. No need to nominate or campaign or even try to go out for anything I'm interested in. She gets the nomination, she is named homecoming representative, she has her picture and is quoted in the school paper. It's as if she speaks for the whole class.

~Lyssa, 15

Dear Dr. Erika:

I'm not a nerd or anything but not slutty either and yet something weird happens to me when I go to a party. Really. It's when everyone—even the top girl in class—starts getting into stuff like beer and cigarettes, you know. Well, I don't want to drink or smoke. But just last weekend I was actually picking up a beer. The only thing that stopped me was this girl's parents showing up.

~Elise, 16

FYI

A Clique Chick is a girl who doesn't make a move without her entourage. That's her train of attendants, followers, gal pals, or co-chicks. Some of them might even be part of *iron* cliques—very tight cliques that formed way back in kindergarten or grade school.

These cliques, iron or not, can consist of one or even several dozen girls. But what they all have in common is that they cluster around a girl who's Miss Popularity because of her looks, or the way she acts, or maybe her material possessions. From elementary school on, the Clique Chick isn't too concerned about grades or sports, although she's into them. Yet mostly she's concerned about herself—her looks, her clothes, her hair, all of her expensive hot stuff. At least that's the way it seems from the outside. But there's no doubt about one thing: The Clique Chick cares about having many, many friends. One or two only? Forget about it!

To rule over her many gal pals, the Clique Chick spends serious time in front of the mirror worrying about what to wear, how to fix her bangs, how not to gain weight. She's almost always high maintenance. That means starting in high school, she has her nails done professionally, her hair high- or low-lighted, and she stresses out over her prom dress far in advance, sometimes years ahead of the actual event.

Super Clique Chicks always have a loyal following. From early on, they spend most of their free time talking to and advising other girls, who're desperately trying to become more like the top chick. They talk about who likes whom, who will ask whom for a date, and who should get invited to the next party. It's often a *he said, she said* chitchat, with the *betas* reporting to the *alpha* what's being said.

Any true Clique Chick is the center of many other girls' attention, and naturally she can be harsh in dealing with the members of her clique and other girls. She can decree who's in and who's out, and there's no appealing her decision. What's being said about others isn't important.

Actually cliques are the gathering of girls who can't yet stand on their own two feet. For them, there's safety in numbers. It's like a fab family, especially for girls who feel unloved at home or think no one cares. And the top Clique Chick comes from a similar home situation. Maybe she's an only child with busy parents who have their attention elsewhere. Or she comes from a background that's not demonstrative and doesn't show warmth, so the clique queen has to get it from her court.

And whatever the alpha chick's age, she has picked up adult characteristics prematurely. Often she's fifteen going on twenty-five. The reason is that she's a pseudo grown-up on the one hand; on the other, she's way immature. She wants a sisterhood swarming around her to make up for the attention she lacks. Even though she had to grow up fast, she has a childlike values system. She thinks clothes and nails and hair are what life's all about. And yet deep down, she's loving and caring—but also trying so hard to make up for what's missing, that often she turns even her own mom, sisters, and aunts into her entourage. Her frequent Barbie-doll appearance reinforces her status. So, overall, a Clique Chick is a girl who has alpha status and can—at times—be extremely mean, rude, or cutting.

First Person: What Happened at the Prom—A Real Life Story
(as told by a teacher)

. . . The girls swept into the immaculately decorated gym by different doors. Both were accompanied by their big-man-on-campus boyfriends *du jour* and several other less popular couples. As they advanced toward each other, a huge pall fell over the lively party. Prior to that moment, at least five hundred kids and numerous teachers and parent chaperones had been dancing, drinking punch, and talking animatedly about which girl would be named prom queen that night.

Now a palpable gloom brought everything, even the expensive big band, to a screeching halt. Why?

Because these two super Clique Chicks were wearing the same elaborate designer prom dress in the same vivid color—aquamarine. Plus, their long blond hair was coifed in the exact same elegant up-do. What was worse: Even their nails and eye shadow—a frosty pale blue—was the same, as were their three-inch spaghetti-strap silver sandals.

What a total disaster. Only their wrist corsages were different, but not much. One was made of white-blue orchids matching the nail polish and eye shadow. The other was made of white-silver orchids matching the sandals.

And then what happened? The Clique Chicks stopped five feet from each other and stared.

Finally, the festivities started again, tentatively at first. The band picked up, the other kids started moving again, but everyone's head craned as they kept looking at the "twins." That meant the party began to drag. It was like a layer of molasses had been poured on the shiny dance floor, making the dancers slog along, while their mouths were at a fevered pitch, taking sides with their favorite "twin." Soon here and there, threats began to rise like wisps of smoke. Some of the other girls started heading for the punch bowl vowing to be the first to throw a cup of punch on their "enemy's" gown, while some of the boys were starting to vent their anger on the enemy's innocent date.

In order to prevent any fights from breaking out, the prom had to be closed down and everyone went home. But neither the girls nor anyone else present ever forgot the "Prom That Wasn't." How could they?

First Rate: Grade the Girls

C- Because the other girls and the rest of the people in attendance folded without giving it a good try anyway. All of them should have sent the jealous chicks and their chums packing, cleaned house, and then had the social event of the century.

Instead, the teachers and chaperones overreacted, but who can totally blame them? They were afraid that after the unfortunate occurrence, the prom wouldn't have worked. And the longer the competing twin queens were in the same room, the closer the situation came to getting out of hand. While there wasn't much chance of the top Clique Chicks getting into a fight, their entourage was on the verge of trading licks. And in order to prevent that, the prom was cancelled.

‹FAST QUIZ›

Clique Lit—Are You a Clique Chick?

Isn't it a shame that so many other kids missed out on their prom because of two girls? You can help put a stop to this type of behavior by empowering yourself against Clique Chicks.

So ask yourself now: Are you susceptible to any Clique Chick tricks? Let's take a quiz and find out:

1. Senior Skip Day has long been a tradition at your school. Only one problem—you're not a senior yet! Still, the *alpha* girl in

your grade and all her attendants and friends have decided to observe Skip Day, too, this year. You:

a. Make sure you sneeze and cough several times during class before the "Skip Day," so you can "legitimately" stay home nursing your li'l 'ole cold and won't have to be out in the cruel world. Better to hide than have to decide where you stand on ditching class.

b. Go wherever the wind blows you. If you have a class with some people who are skipping, you talk as if you're going to skip, too. If you run into a group of friends who thinks skipping is dumb, you agree with them—uh-uh, no way, skipping is stupid!

c. Don't let the Clique Chick dictate when you cut class. Just who does she think she is, anyway? You tell her she's totally unoriginal for skipping on Senior Skip Day. Everyone will know what she's up to, anyway. When you feel like skipping school, you'll skip school—but on her orders? Not on your life!

d. Know what you want in life—major success!—and the prerequisite for that is doing your best in school. Sure, sleeping late and lounging around the house all day is tempting, but you've got a lot to do. Besides, your parents can be super cool about that kind of stuff. In fact, your mom promised you a free day of shopping and movies if you bring your history grade up, and you're saving your "skip day" for that!

2. On a field trip with your advanced biology class to the nearby university, your teacher tells you to carefully check out the world-famous marine lab, then meet for lunch at the student union. The Clique Chick decides that the group should skip the lab and opts instead for a way long lunch. You:

a. Hurry to the bathroom in the marine lab lobby where you hop on the throne and peruse a pamphlet on the exhibits.

That way you're okay with both the clique and the teacher. Aren't you smart!

b. Volunteer to "swear" to the teacher that you saw the clique in the exhibit hall with your very own eyes. That means you have to personally stroll through that lame place, but anything to get an in with the ins! Next venture, you won't have to be a "bencher" anymore.

c. Skip the morning lab plus the afternoon junk—a lecture on the Jacques Cousteau Institute—as well, and hang out with a couple of hot college guys. And if that Barbie-doll diva or any of her devotees opens her trap, you'll spill it about what they were doing all afternoon.

d. Check out the exhibit. Let the Clique Chick and her crew play their baby games. You've got no use for them. Hey, marine biology stuff may not be your bag, but at least it's a day out of school. Besides, even though English lit is more your style, some of it's interesting, anyway. Might as well scope it out while you're here.

3. At the end-of-the-year class picnic, everyone's participating in silly games—such as the three-legged sack race, the water balloon fight, the rope pulling, and the egg toss—for which points are allotted to the participants. You and your group are desperately trying to win the huge trophy, and you do! Afterward, when you and the rest of your friends look over the tally sheet, you notice that somebody made a mistake in adding up the scores. You and your clique actually came in second. Ouch! You:

a. Inch away and make sure to help out with cleaning up the picnic grounds. Score keeping isn't on your menu, really, so why fret?

b. You just happen to have a pen in the exact color of the one used on the tally sheet. And then you offer to make an 8 out of the 3. No one will even notice, your team will win, and you'll be the cool chick of the day!

c. Talk about life being unfair! Your team tried sooo hard, even if some of the girls on your team were shorter, while the other teams had these hefty mamas. Did you see some of those girls? They looked like they should be auditioning for professional wrestling, not participating in the three-legged race! For sure, they were stronger teams, but why change your score now? What's done is done, right? Obviously, whoever added it up came to their senses and gave your team plus-points. Big deal!

d. Recheck the scores slowly, then—no matter how much you hate doing it—show the mistake to your teammates, then take it to the picnic supervisors. Let them handle the problem. It's such a bummer you have to give back the trophy, but your team had a blast in the competitions, anyway. Despite your stripped gold medal and some slightly wounded egos, you manage to rally the girls together for ice cream sundaes—a soul soother if ever there was one!

4. When the yearbooks come out, you and your group have an autograph session and discuss what's going to be different in next year's annual. The leader in your group suggests that the senior superlative section needs help. Besides the usual Best Dressed, Best Grades, Best Athletes, Most Likely to Succeed, and Best All-Around categories, your class should start a new trend and vote for Worst Dressed, Worst Grades, Worst Athletes, Most Likely to Flunk, and Total Moron. Everybody just loves the idea—what a riot!—and they start tossing around the names of classmates that were born for the new categories. You:

a. Cringe in fear, hoping and praying that nobody mentions your name in connection with any of the new superlatives! Okay, so not everyone can be on top of her fashion game, and maybe you could use some coaching on your fast-pitch softball game, but is that any reason to be labeled for all eternity as a loser?

b. Hustle to act as super secretary, taking stellar notes and joining in enthusiastically. By being an active participant, you're hoping to score major bonus points with the leader of the group and your faculty sponsor. So what if a few losers get labeled in the process? As long as it's not you, you're fine with whatever the group wants.

c. Think it's a horrible idea, and you speak your mind. You're usually not out to label anyone, but just to even the score, you suggest to the leader that you just thought of two categories she'd be perfect for—Most Shallow and Tackiest Attitude.

d. Feel uncomfortable with the new superlatives, and you let the group know about it. The purpose of the yearbook is to remind your class of good memories, not bad ones. Who wants to be remembered by a class that would vote for such rude categories, anyway? As an alternative, you suggest a new section of funny superlatives for some of the most popular teachers just to lighten things up a bit.

Answers

Now it's time to find out how you did. Total up your answers.

3 or 4 A's
check out Answer 1.

3 or 4 C's
check out Answer 3.

3 or 4 B's
check out Answer 2.

3 or 4 D's
check out Answer 4.

If you have a mixture of A's, B's, C's, and D's, look at all the answers. Obviously, there's a little bit of everything in you, which is great. Now can you work on getting a little more of that Answer # 4 attitude?

1. The Clique Chicklet

You may not be the alpha chick in your group, but you're definitely guilty of being a chicklet. When are you going to realize that your opinions mean something and that expressing them is powerful? There's nothing in the girl world that you can't handle. Just take a deep breath and face your fear factor. Stand up to those other girls! You deserve better than living in their shadows, and it's time you did the right thing for you.

2. Group Groupie

You're so anxious to gain attention and be part of the group that you sacrifice yourself to be part of the popular chick landscape. Next time, stop and think before you rush to cater to the whims of the Clique Chick and her crew. Why are you doing this? Do you really need their approval that badly? Here's a tip: Try pleasing yourself for a change, rather than trying so hard to please others. The world is at your fingertips. All you have to do is reach out and grab it.

3. In the Mood for 'Tude

The good news is that you're an energetic action girl. While your intentions may start off on the right foot, the bad news is that you may be misapplying your energy and in loose-cannon style. Expressing your opinion is great, but as they say, "Timing is everything." Next time, give your brain a chance to shift into high gear before you spring into action. If you do that, you're almost sure to gain the respect of your classmates. You are a smart girl, and you have lots of good things to offer the girl world. But first things first—get a grip on that lip! You may be hurting others when you're only trying to help.

4. Alpha Who???

You have good self-esteem and know how to handle yourself when confronted with Clique Chicks with mean tricks up their sleeve. One of those mean tricks is to try to get you to fold under pressure, peer pressure, that is. But you're not folding; you are holding on to your good values. And by your great example, even some other girls can learn to be strong.

 If all the girls in our school would get together in one <u>caring</u> clique, just think of how much we could get done.
—Jewel, 14

Clique Chick Smarts—What Should You Know about the Clique Chick?

Here's a list of things to keep in mind about the Clique Chick:

⭐ Know that mean clique conduct often involves putting the *clique squeeze*, otherwise known as peer pressure, on you. Peer pressure can bring out either the best or the worst in you. All you have to do is examine it and ask: What are your peers really pressuring you to do?

⭐ At first, clique squeeze might seem pretty harmless, like how you dress or wear your hair. While part of "finding yourself" can mean going along with the pack, be sure to watch your back around this type of behavior. First, it may only be clothes or hair, but that can expand into other things, like who you can and can't date or even being cruel to other girls. Don't get caught up in that type of game. Keep yourself safe, and always be true to your goals and your soul.

⭐ So focus on yourself, your talents, and your potential. Rather than spending your energy on trying to please the alphas or betas, be the strong gamma you are and do what enhances your own life and what contributes to *your* fabulous future.

 A girl who's strong and says <u>no</u> to whatever's bad for her gets to be a leader for other girls, and then it's like a brush fire. It spreads and spreads. —Melody, 16

Rapid Response: What You Should Do about the Clique Chick

Follow these steps to guard against the Clique Chicks:

1. Fight the *clique squeeze* at your school just by giving the ruling clique of chicks at your school the cold shoulder. Be independent-minded and develop your own style.

 In high school the most common reason for excluding you from a top clique is when a girl doesn't look a certain way. So a lot of girls like really starve themselves. That's bad, but that's just the way it is! ～Pretty, 15

2. Stop worrying about what other girls want you to do and just be yourself. Did you know that "popular" actually means average or ordinary? Don't strive so hard to be just ordinary. Be extraordinary. Be outstanding!

3. Try sharing some of these tricks on dealing with cliques with other girls—maybe your little sister and her friends or even girls in grades lower than you. Tell a teacher that you and your friends want to volunteer, and talk to younger girls and help them survive in the girl world. By teaching others how to be strong, you are allowing your own strength to grow.

 Reach for a higher power! That's what I do every day, really. I pray for the girls who try to get other girls to do what they're not supposed to do, and I pray for the girls who are tempted. ～Cathy, 17

Fab Fixes for Whatever Attitude Ails You

Now more so than ever, fashion plays a key role in our society. Just look at television, magazines, and billboards—it's practically all you see! You know, every time you turn around, fashions can change from way wow to way yuck in a matter of weeks. Naturally, it's fun to get together with your girls and talk fashion. But, unless you're Madonna, it's nearly impossible to keep up with every fad. Think about it—trying out tons of new things can be super fun. It helps you learn about what you like and don't like. In other words, it helps you learn more about you. Whether the fad you're trying on is fashion or music or lifestyle, you're always learning, right? But in your quest for the best, what if you get too caught up in the latest and the greatest and forget about the "you" that's really inside. Sure, your new shoes match your new purse and they're totally hot! But what happens when your fashion attitude becomes Fad-itude?

How should you deal with it?

Rx—Facing Up to Fad-itude

Just keep the following in mind:

1. Know that fads are great fun if they're not overdone. If it's in your budget and looks great on you and if your mom approves, then it's the thing to do. So go ahead and get a pair of those hot new sunglasses or some new glittery nail polish. (Never mind your little brother who declares that puce toenails make him want to puke! What does he know about fashion, anyway?)

2. Fads can be fab, but don't follow them blindly. Pick and choose what to try and what to buy. And make sure that whatever you choose makes a statement about you—who you are and who you want to be. One of the greatest things about fashion is individuality. Don't lose yours just to keep up with the race.

3. With so much to worry about, it's easy to forget about stuff. Next time you go crazy because you just have to have that new pair of jeans and nothing else will do, give yourself a reality check, girl! No matter what fad you're following this week, don't forget to be giving to others. What about all of those clothes you don't wear anymore? Instead of letting them take up room in your closet, why not donate them to a local clothing drive or Salvation Army store? Doing good deeds for others can be just as fun as doing good deeds for yourself.

So, enjoy yourself as you predict the next big fashion forecast. But remember, always be grateful, always be gracious. When it's all said and done, do you want someone to remember you for what you wore or for what gifts you gave to the world?

The Bottom Line

So, what's the bottom line on Clique Chicks and their fad-itudes? Read on:

* Fads don't last, they fade. So next time you feel yourself getting caught up in a fad, step back. You're in charge. Do what you want, be who you like—just make sure you're being true to yourself.

* Before getting involved with any group or clique, be sure to ask yourself, "What makes this clique tick?" If it's for friendship or a worthy cause, embrace it. But if it's all for show, step back and think a minute before you make that swan dive. Remember, *popular* means ordinary, not extraordinary.

* If a certain mean chick and her clique are getting you down, then you can get out. Who needs to be around a leader who's a loser? You're growing, you're becoming more "you" each and every day. Don't let any Clique Chick stand in the way of how smart, original, and funny you really are.

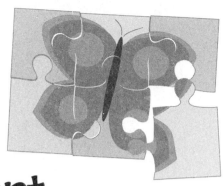

Part III

Empowerment Strategies

 lways remember: You are here on earth as the latest, most advanced model of the human race. You truly are the hottest design to come off the awesome human assembly line. So you have within yourself all the seeds to do even more, to *be* even more, than anyone before! All you have to do is *flex your girl power to survive, strive, and thrive!* How?

By realizing just how *powerful*, *wonderful*, and *beautiful* you really are, no matter what you look like.

So when you're asked the question:

 Tell me honestly, is it the nature of girls to be unkind to each other? ⌒ Cherie, 13

you can answer like Aimee:

 No, it's not. What we have to do is give each girl power <u>another</u> way. ⌒ Aimee, 14

What also helps is getting together with friends who feel similar to the way we do: My mother and grandmother always told me to treat people like you want to be treated. I follow that rule all the time, because I don't want someone to feel bad about herself because of me. That's not cool. So I hang <u>only</u> with girls who feel the same way as me. ⌒ Silvia, 17

Chapter 8

The Power of One

Words to Live By: Every girl can make a difference! All you need is the Power of One! ~Erika Karres

What Is the Power of One?

Well, you're about to find out. But first, here's a clue—it starts with you! All it takes is *one* girl to change the climate in your school and do something about this mean chick behavior we've been hearing so much about. Sure, we all know that boys can be mean, too. But it seems that our schools are better equipped to deal with their behavior. In fact, teachers pass on information about which boys tend to fight from grade to grade. Therefore, administrators and counselors keep a special eye on them and make sure the most aggressive boys get placed into classes where they are separated from each other. Plus, in some school systems, boys known for their temper outbursts are put into courses such as weight-lifting, where they can work off some steam. Or they are especially monitored and given privileges such as being named assistants in PE or serving as aides in the office.

Truth be told, whole school communities band together to remove any triggers or inconveniences from potentially violent boys. And numerous teachers tiptoe around them, while everyone heaves a sigh of relief when those boys, known to be bullies, act relatively peaceful.

But nobody ever seems to make any special allowances for girls who go off like a time bomb. With your help, all of that can change. All you have to do is discover . . . the Power of One.

Dear Dr. Erika:

When I first started middle school, other girls picked on me because of my size, just because I was a little bigger than they were. At that age, I didn't know anything about wearing only the name-brand clothes or anything about the word "skinny." That was the last thing on my mind. I was just ready for recess so I could go outside and play with my friends. I don't remember what I did to stand up for myself or how getting called names affected me mentally, but I will always remember the harsh words and I felt the emotional pain from it.

Today I know how to stand up for myself very well. I do not let things get to me as easily as I used to, and I do not give the smaller worries a bigger shadow. I try to be myself, and doing that has gotten me further than anything.

And I'm proud to say that my waist size has no effect on my self-esteem at all! Most important, I try to surround myself with girls who are positive and who set goals for themselves and their future. I think that's the best way—keeping away from girls that say negative comments about others.

In the end you learn to be an all-around nice person.

~Shea, 16

FYI

In most teacher texts—books teachers use to study educational theory in college—aggressive girls rate no more than a sentence or two. Especially since the Columbine High School tragedy, it's boys, boys, boys who get the most attention when it comes to preventing violent outbursts in school.

But just because girls don't often duke it out physically—pow! pow! pow!—and come to school toting a gun, that doesn't mean they don't have feelings: feelings of disappointment, of anger, and of rage. Also just because girls in general seem to hold in their negative emotions better, that doesn't mean that schools should simply overlook them.

But they often do, and that makes the discontent simmer below the surface of the girl world. In other words, it's there but it hasn't been openly acknowledged. Until now. Until you picked up this book.

So now focus on yourself. Think about yourself and all you can do, all that's in you. My, how much there is—what a wealth of abilities you have. You can think and talk, have opinions, change your mind, ponder this and that, and ponder it some more the next day.

Rapid Response—What You Can Do to Promote the Power of One

Try this for promoting the Power of One:

1. Be sure that you're doing well. Are you happy? Are you content with your grades? There's always going to be a class or two that makes you groan every time you think about it. What a great place to start with the Power of One! Set a goal. Give yourself a challenge and rise to achieve it. Maybe it's as small as making sure you get your homework done every night. Or maybe it's as large as acing that final. Remember, it's not a competition. These are your goals and yours alone. Just be sure to do your best, no matter what.

2. Then think about your life outside school. There's a whole world out there for you to explore. What are you doing when you're not in school? Are you having fun, getting exercise, hanging with your buds? With so many things to do in school every day, it's easy to forget that one of the best parts of being a girl is kicking back and having a good time. Be sure to work some fun into your schedule. You'll thank yourself for it later.

3. Are you helping others both in and out of school? Maybe it's time to think about some volunteer activities that help your community. How about volunteering for a nature project? Or what about helping out at the local center for the arts? By lending a helping hand to your classmates and your community, you are helping to spread positive power through the girl world and beyond.

Whatever you attack first, remember you really are a power-house of one. But before you can change anything for the better, sometimes you may have to straighten out something that's not so nice about yourself, like Ginnie did.

When I started junior high, I was very skinny but had plenty of friends. I hung out with the popular girl clique and got along with everyone. Only one time did I get in trouble. That was when one of my friends kept calling me "Stick." Stick this, and Stick that.

One day I couldn't take it anymore. I had had enough. I just snapped. I just threw this girl down, jumped on top of her, and started hitting her in the face. The teachers ran over, pulled me off of her, and proceeded to take me to the office. Somehow, I managed to get loose and jumped back on top of her again. I felt so much better after that. I couldn't wipe the smile off my face and had no regrets about the trouble I was in because this was the first time I had ever defended myself.

The next year I gained weight but my parents got divorced and I was depressed 24/7. I wanted things back the way they used to be. Nobody knew what was going on because I didn't want anyone to know. I didn't know how to handle all the emotions I was feeling, so I lashed out at everyone. I turned into a real brat, acted like I was better than everybody, and stomped my foot when things didn't go my way. I slammed doors, and I also did the name calling, the teasing, and the rumor spreading. I acted like a real *$?&!. One teacher noticed it and sent me to the school counselor and I told her about my issues.

From then on every week she checked up on me. She would always tell me if I felt real bad or mad or depressed to come talk to her about it first before doing anything. She said I had to learn about what made me so down and angry and how to deal with it. Her invitation and knowing that she was there for me if no one else was saved me.

~Ginnie, 18

So, you see how Ginnie empowered herself? She didn't like the way she was acting, so she got some help. By talking to the school guidance counselor about her problems, she realized she wasn't alone and that she was stronger than she thought. She started dealing with her sadness over her parents' divorce and realized that taking it out on her classmates was not the way to go.

First Person: What I Realized—A Real Life Story

I remember when it started, me picking on this girl. It was the beginning of middle school, and this girl was one I couldn't stand. She was short but not too short, nor too tall. She had long black hair and she was skinny.

One time I poured some ice water on her T-shirt, and she had to stay at school with a wet T-shirt all day because she couldn't call home. Another time I put a toad frog down her pants. Once when we were in class I had to sit behind her, and I stuck some gum in her hair.

One day we went on a class trip to the skating rink, and I took a pair of skates and told her she could wear them. She didn't have much money, so I acted like I was helping her out.

But, see, the night before, I loosened the screws in the wheels on the skates. So when she started to skate, the wheels came off and she fell and busted her butt. She wasn't badly hurt, but she was hurting pretty badly. I felt sorry for doing that, and I apologized to her and told her to keep it quiet. But she didn't, and I got suspended from school for a week. Man, did my mom tear my backside up for days.

When I went back to school that next week, some of my friends told me that the girl's mother had just died and everybody was showing her sympathy.

But guess who wasn't showing her sympathy? Me.

Still I left her alone for two weeks. After that, she came up to me and said she wanted me to stop picking on her. Please! I said okay and she walked off, at which point I tapped her on the shoulder. When she turned around, I struck her in her face.

To my surprise, she hit me back. Both of us got into trouble for that, but I got in more because I threw the first lick. Plus, I hadn't realized how strong she had gotten over the years. Otherwise, I would have left her alone.

If I had, I'd still have my *real* front teeth in my mouth!

~Rikki Lee, 15

P.S.: What I learned was that *I had a problem* that I needed to work on, which I did. Now I try to make friends with every girl I meet.

First Rate: Grade the Girls

A! Good job, Rikki Lee, for realizing the problem was you. And for then having the courage to work on it. But this grade is *only* for how you ended up and *not* for how you started out, which was *very* cruel.

Smart Strategies

Now it's time to look at some smart strategies to get you through the day. These strategies come from real girls all over the country—girls just like you. Check out what they have to say.

Smart Strategy #1

 Once I was picked on by this girl about my weight. She said I eat nasty things that I would never eat. So I was thinking: Why don't we start a girls' workout club and hand out nutrition info at every school? ~Caryn, 13

Caryn has a good point. A healthy body and mind go hand in hand. It's medically proven that just thirty minutes of exercise a few times a week is not only good for your body, it's also good for your mood. It can improve your focus, your mood, and even your sleeping patterns. Perhaps if the girls at your school had a workout club, they would feel better about themselves, which means they don't have the need to tease each other. Then, rather than competing about clothes, cliques, or gossip, girls can compete through sports, which is much more healthy for your mind—and your body!

Why not try to form a workout club in your own school? Check with your PE teacher or someone else you trust and find out what you can do to get a club like this going in your own school. If working out isn't your thing, there are tons of clubs you could organize—maybe a roller-blading club, a literary magazine, or even a game club where girls could get together in teams and play games.

Smart Strategy #2

I have picked on another girl before but it was like we were cracking jokes on each other. I know it's not right to <u>pick</u> on anyone. So why don't we have a short course, like a couple hours at the beginning of every school year where they teach us the difference? ⌒ Rene, 15

Great idea, Rene. The difference between harmless teasing and hurling hateful words should be taught, and not just at your school but everywhere the world over. Talk to a teacher or maybe even your principal about having a course like this. Or, if you like, maybe you can start such a program yourself.

"Me," you say? Yes, you. You know you've got the Power of One.

Start by going to the librarian at your school and tell her what you have in mind. She can network with other school librarians and order books or pamphlets on this topic for you. Also check with your guidance counselor and ask for his or her help. Then, maybe at the beginning of the school year, you can visit various homerooms or classes and tell them about the course. Or maybe you can pass on information about the topic to teachers and they can use it as part of class discussion. Education is power, and by educating your peers about the ways of mean chicks, who knows, you could be the start of a wonderful change.

Or, if having a class is not your thing, maybe you can institute a Planned Acts of Kindness Day. Talk to your teachers about having a day that promotes girl-to-girl kindness and awareness of mean chick behavior.

Smart Strategy #3

It's wrong to pick on girls to hurt their feelings, so why don't our teachers make us stop it? Why aren't there any rules posted about it? You know, like in the halls, in the gym, and on the buses. And why don't we have announcements over the intercom every day, with messages like:

- Bullyproof Our School! Or,
- Bullying Isn't Cool; It's 4 Fools. Or,
- Watching someone being bullied is bad for you. It means, you're a bully, too.

Stuff like that would really help. ⁓ Megan, 14

Until there is a way for girls to speak out against obstacles such as gossiping, rumors, and namecalling, there won't be a solution to the problem.

So be sure to use some of Megan's suggestions or create some of your own. There are tons of fun ways to express yourself through art, so why not use it to help improve the girl world?

First, get permission to post signs and banners on the walls. Then, put your head together with some friends or classmates and create a message that's impossible to ignore. Create posters, banners, flyers, maybe even draw a cartoon for your school's newspaper.

Work up a "Warning: This Is a Bully-Free Zone" poster, then make copies and tack them on the bulletin boards of every classroom.

Talk to the teacher you admire the most; get her input on a creative handout you could come up with on the types and warning signs of girls' aggressiveness. Then pass it out, after getting the okay from the school administration first, of course.

By using some of these Smart Strategies or by creating your own, you are empowering yourself and passing that power on to other girls who need it. You're moving and improving your surroundings. Good for you!

Fab Fixes for Whatever Attitude Ails You

Some days you wake up, hear the sounds of your family members moving through the house, maybe somewhat sleepily, and you jump up beating them to everything—the bathroom, the kitchen, the newspaper on the driveway. Oh, this is a day you feel you can move mountains. That's how good you feel. Nothing can stop you, not even the thought of a long and tough schedule ahead.

So really, you know you can do it and do it well, or at least as well as you can, which is great. It means you have a case of can-do attitude—wow! That's the right attitude to have. It's easy to put into action because it's built on what you already have so much of—your aptitude.

So reinforce it. How? Just use this prescription tailored to you:

Rx—Amping Up Your Aptitude

Do 3x a day:

1. Repeat out loud (when you're alone): "I can and will make a difference!"
2. Lie on top of your bed, close your eyes, and envision yourself succeeding in life. Imagine that you can accomplish anything you want. And especially imagine what you can do to help your school to become free of mean chick behavior.
3. Start a girl-to-girl kindness chain. Choose the most "blah" day at your school, like Mondays. Then decide that on this day you say only nice things to other girls and about them. And then encourage your friends to do the same. Just have this *one day a week* be totally free of backbiting, gossiping, teasing, and cutting down other girls. Think of how many other girls you can help. Wow!

The Bottom Line

So, what's the bottom line on the Power of One?

★ You have so much power inside you. Think about it and be grateful to be who you are. Then use it—this awesome power. It's such a great feeling to use your Power of One for yourself and for others.

★ Start with a small project that represents that Power of One that you have; next time, tackle a bigger problem and just think of how many girls will benefit from what you're doing.

★ Then aim for something even bigger to do—something you can spend some time on, maybe something that will change an outdated school rule, or add a new one, update a program, or start a new one. Use all your creativity and your smarts, those in your head and in your heart!

Check out how Anna Liu overcame her problems and worked to make a difference:

When I was thirteen I had to wear glasses because I am nearsighted. At first I was really excited about having glasses. I went to the doctor's office to pick them up. I tried them on to make sure they fit and they did! I began to get numerous compliments from the doctors and even people I had never met. My confidence rose to the extreme.

When I returned to school that following Monday, before I could reach my classroom I began to hear laughter and hear my classmates shouting, "Is that her with those glasses?"

I just knew they were referring to me, but I didn't let it get to me at first. But as the day went on, the laughing got worse. I lost my sense of coping and started to cry. This one girl in particular looked at me and said, "Stop crying, you already look a mess!"

In anger I snatched the glasses off and broke them. I had taken all the embarrassment that I could take for one day. When I got home, my mother asked me where my glasses were.

"Broke," I said. "Nobody liked them and people made fun of me. They laughed and called me names. I don't ever want to wear glasses again."

After my mother embraced me and explained to me that no matter what people thought about my new look I would always be beautiful, my mother called the eye doctor and made an appointment to get brand-new glasses.

That next week I had a new attitude about my glasses and I didn't care what people said or thought! And then I wrote about it for my school paper, and several other girls came up and said they saved this issue because it helped them when they were teased. Now they knew they were not alone. Yippee, I didn't know a little old essay of mine could do so much good. I mean it was just me doing it.

~Anna Liu, 14

Chapter 9

The Power of Several

Words to Live By: Courage is very important. Like muscle, it is strengthened by use. ~Ruth Gordon

What Is the Power of Several?

"You know what would really be great?" one of the girls I interviewed for this book asked me.

She had my full attention: "No, what?"

"If we could start a Newcomers Club at every school. This club would be for all girls new to the school and also for those girls wanting to show them the ropes. And even during times when no new girls would enroll, this club could still meet and plan stuff that would make every girl enjoy school more."

"It would be a *real chat room.*"

FYI

That's a great idea. So scout around your school and try to see if you can find a space somewhere where you and other girls interested in a real chat room could meet. Perhaps there is a large closet that's not being used, or a classroom that's not used at lunch. With permission, you could meet there twice a week. Or just designate a table in the cafeteria and hold your informal but oh-so-helpful chats there.

Just think of all you can do or are thinking of doing to make your school less unkind.

 Picking or teasing others at school or anyplace else is definitely wrong and should be stopped cold. It's like a cancer that grows every day. So if it happens to you or if you observe it going on, do something before it's too late.
〜Lara, 13

What can help lots is to give more girl-to-girl support. And then multiply that by ten or twenty. That's exactly how much a small or mid-sized group of girls can accomplish. For cliques can be positive and not just negative. As a matter of fact, one truly good clique can overcome any number of sick ones.

A good clique is one devoted to helping girls reach their potential as individuals and as a group. Being with such a girl clique is uplifting and inspiring. It helps girls achieve their best, in the classroom, on the swim team, or at the track conference meet. These girls are great chicks who will cheer and clap for each other, spurring one another on to new heights.

Always get the best that's inside you out, in track, volleyball, gymnastics, or swimming, whatever. That's how you can really overcome whomever (or whatever) tries to make you less and set an example for others.
〜Martina, 17

What being with other power girls truly does is to bring out and reinforce the best in each and every one. It's like one steady candle burning on a dark night. It makes a little light, but when you add several more candles burning brightly, you have enough to get rid of the gloom and shadows.

So girls doing good things for each other can start an avalanche of positive change for other girls.

Rapid Response: What You Can Do to Promote the Power of Several

Try these for taking advantage of the Power of Several:

1. Get together with your friends and discuss the biggest "girl world" problem at your school. Some schools have more girl teasing; others have more gossiping going on. Still others have a combination of mean chick behavior. Just broach the topic with your group and see what the upshot is. Once you identify the main problem, you're that much closer to finding a solution.

2. Talk about how powerful girls can be. Know that you owe it to yourself to strive for the best you can be. Realize that it's okay to be different. Find strength in your differences and identify the special potential that your group has to bring about change.

3. Be friends with girls from various segments of your school. Power resides among the shy girls, the new girls, the girls that nobody talks to. Just how much power and talent and strength lies in each of your classmates will emerge once you and your group befriend them, so do it.

First Person: How We Made a Difference—A Real Life Story

This is the story of a little girl back in middle school who got picked on all the time. She was overweight and wore clothes that weren't in style. There were all these preppy girls in our classes that would make fun of her to her face and behind her back, move from tables at lunch because she sat down, and spread rumors about her saying she had a nasty disease. They tormented this poor girl for years. She developed a speech problem and went to a therapy class during school and they made fun of that, too.

But she never said anything back to these girls. She always just sat there, so quiet and sweet, and just took it. Rumor after rumor was made up about her. Yet she never reacted to the bully girls even though you could tell that it was hurting her so badly deep down inside. It must have been like a nightmare to wake up every single morning, knowing she had to face that over and over again, like she had for the longest time.

She really was the sweetest girl you could ever imagine, and I felt horrible that she got picked on so much. I and two of my friends always tried to be kind to her and even stood up for her and sat with her when no one else would. We volunteered to be her partner in some of our classes because no one else would do it. To this day, we're still friends with this girl and have introduced her to some of the new friends we've made.

I think she has a happier life now. And I'm so glad we helped her.

~ *Emily, 18*

First Rate: Grade the Girls

A++ Congratulations to you, Emily, and to your friends for taking this girl under your wings. Whether you realized it or not, you were exhibiting the Power of Several. It took loads of courage to stand up for her and heaps of kindness to be her partner in class. By taking that step and setting a good example, other girls will learn to follow your lead.

Smart Strategies

Now let's look at some great ways to put the Power of Several into action. There's nobody more capable than an intelligent girl like you. Get together with some of your best pals or classmates and you'll be amazed by what you can accomplish.

Smart Group Strategy #1

Picking on other girls should have its consequences like any other bad behavior. It can lead to hurt feelings, fights, and suspension from school—and it should. But the consequences have to really be spelled out in a student handbook! ~ Aisha, 17

Exactly. Have you ever read your student handbook? How does it handle mean chick behavior? Starting now, *every* school needs to spell out what unacceptable behavior is and that includes not only physical bullying but also calling names, teasing, spreading rumors, and gossiping.

So quick, pull out the student handbook of your school. Look for the "code of conduct" section or the "school rules." Then read what it says about those mean behaviors. You'll probably find that most schools only mention physical fighting and cursing, and then give the cold shoulder to the other (and oftentimes even worse) mean behaviors.

 No girl can really say there hasn't been a point in her life when she didn't pick on someone. The reason is that nobody ever teaches girls that <u>it is wrong</u>. ⌒ Cyndi, 16

So you and your friends can be the ones to get the message out everywhere: *It's wrong to be a mean chick.* Take your girl power group to the principal's office and voice your concerns. Ask for new rules to be added to the book. It's time to start taking a stand against mean chick behavior!

Smart Group Strategy #2

 I am sure even Laura Bush or Condoleezza Rice picked on someone at one time or another, or they were picked on. So it's way common. But wouldn't it be great if they, or some other well-known female leaders, would come to our school and tell us how we can stop it so the unnecessary pain won't be passed along like some other school traditions? ⌒ Lisa Sun, 15

Yes, that's a great idea. With mean chick behavior so prevalent in the girl world, it would be really great to hear from some super cool women leaders and role models to share their stories and learn from their wisdom.

Get together with your girlfriends and make up a list of women you admire most. Take your list to a trusted teacher or to your principal and let him or her in on your plan. Tell her you think this is an important issue—so important that the whole school should get together to learn about it. Offer to write letters to contact the speakers of your choice, to do Internet searches—whatever it takes. You never know what might come out of it. Never underestimate the power of several smart chicks who are determined to change the world!

Extra Credit: While you're surfing the Net looking for cool speakers to come to your school, why not hop on your school's Web page? Check it out to see if there's a place or a link on the site designated for problem solving and referrals? In other words: Is there a way girls can voice and vent their anger and hurt feelings and report any incidents of mean behavior to a teacher, administrator, or guidance counselor that will be read at once and *followed up on?*

If not, get to work on it. Find out who's in charge of the Web site and tell him or her what's missing. What a thrill for you and your friends to make your school's home page truly and helpfully interactive.

Smart Group Strategy #3

Get together with your friends and set up a help-line, like on the Net, or hand out the phone number of the guidance department. Or start a peer group or a teen court—any avenue you can think of, even if it means inviting powerless girls to unload on you and your friends via e-mail or instant messaging. <u>Don't stop until the teasing stops!</u> ～Terry, 14

Terry has a really great idea. There is strength and safety in numbers, and by forming a help network with your friends and maybe even a trusted teacher or two, you'll be able to reach out and help those who are in pain.

If you're a computer genius, design a Web page that allows girls from your school to discuss the mean chick issues that bug them the most. Maybe you can even get the school counselor to do a weekly advice column to help address some of the larger issues. A little imagination goes a long way, so don't underestimate the power of your ideas!

Fab Fixes for Whatever Attitude Ails You

There are times when all of us see the glass half empty instead of half full, right? Or maybe you open your closet and see nothing but tired and lame outfits and shoes that ought to take a hike—and you're not even talking about your boots!

Yeah, right, some days you wake up so darn critical of yourself and your life. And you feel nothing you do is right and your friends aren't so hot either. Pretty soon, you're swimming in a sea of doubt. That's the moment when you need to dig deep inside you and pull out your secret weapon—the best attitude that there is, and that's *magnitude*.

Wow, once your *magnitude* comes to the forefront, nothing can stop you and your friends. Doesn't matter what's ahead—an obstacle or a decision or a way big problem, whatever. When you and your girl friends use your magnitude to help others, you will prevail. Magnitude means, you guessed it, greatness! And greatness is your birthright. You and your group have it inside of you, so bring it out and use it.

Rx—Maximizing Your Magnitude

Always keep in mind the following:

1. Remember that greatness is in you. Magnitude has nothing to do with brains or brawn or being big or boisterous. But it has everything to do with listening to your heart and acting your best. It means thinking of consequences *before* you do something. It's not rushing in but reasoning out.
2. Think of all the various choices you have, and resolve to

always choose the *high* road, even though it might be the *toughest course* to success. Acting in the spirit of magnitude is reaching positively for the stars, being the most wonderful girl you can be, trying your utmost in class, at home, and in your neighborhood. It's sharing and being generous and upbeat, and biting your tongue when it would've been so much fun to repeat that slur you heard, that juicy bit of gossip, because it was way funny.

3. Let it stop with you. Don't let mean chick behavior get past you any longer. Because now you're in the know. You know the harm that can come from being mean to another girl. So help other girls, be they the targets or the tormentors.

The Bottom Line

The bottom line about standing up to meanness among your circle of girls is the following:

★ Having power includes having *courage*, and you do. You've read and worked through this book because you dare to care and to be courageous.

 I keep a picture of a bird floating on a wind current high above everything by my bed, with this message: Dare to Soar. ∼ Lisa Liu, 14

★ Know that within you, you have such awesome strength that you can do just about anything you want, and then some. By banding together with other strong and independent-minded girls like you, you can multiply your girl power and accomplish more than you ever imagined.

★ The changes you and your girl pals instigate will begin to change the mean chicks atmosphere into a great chicks atmosphere everywhere. You are the first to spread an encouraging environment for all girls.

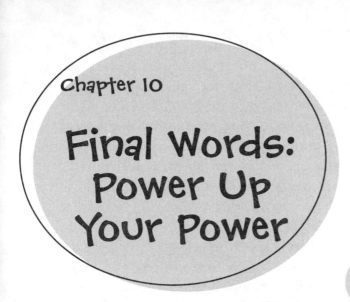

Chapter 10

Final Words: Power Up Your Power

Words to Live By: The door of opportunity won't open unless you do some pushing. ~Anonymous

Now that you're empowered and in charge, not even the sky is the limit! You can do anything you want! By reading this book and taking action, you have provided yourself with so many new choices. Your life ahead will be one of growth, contribution, and unlimited potential.

Now you understand what kind of mean girl behavior can get in your way. And you know how to get around it or over it or how to swat it out of the way like an annoying insect. You are able to spot, analyze, and handle any signs of mean chicks from now on. Hopefully, by reading this book and keeping up with your journal, you've learned more about who you are each and every day and you'll continue to do so.

You're learning to make smart decisions and to stand up for yourself. You're not influenced by the behaviors of others. You are your own girl—and you rule. You are the girl of today, and you have the power to make change happen. There are girls all over the world who would give anything to be in your shoes, so be their heroine, okay?

Always remember to do your best and shine as brightly as you can. You are a mega star, the radiant voice this world needs. You are the youth of today and the idol of tomorrow. Be magnanimous. Be mindful and masterful. Be magnificent every moment, and be proud of the woman you are meant to become.

And always keep in mind that . . .

★ Inside every mean chick is a potentially great chick.
★ Inside *every* girl is the whole world.

Congratulations to you for realizing that, and best wishes!

The Chick List

Here's a great chick list to remind you of what to remember about mean chicks and about yourself as you make your way through the world with smarts and style.

Directions: Place checks next to those items you feel very confident about. Each check is worth 10 points.

1. _____ Can you identify the Snob at your school and not be intimidated by her?
2. _____ Can you spot the Gossip(s) and refuse to be drawn into her gossiping?
3. _____ Can you recognize the Teaser and not be bugged by her?
4. _____ Do you know who the Bully is at your school and can you protect yourself and your friends from her?
5. _____ Can you bounce back after the Traitor has betrayed you without becoming bitter?
6. _____ Do you know where you stand in your group?
7. _____ Do you know what it takes to be a team player?
8. _____ Can you deal with the Clique Chicks at your school?
9. _____ Do you feel powerful and know that just one girl— you!—can make a difference?
10. _____ Do you know that you and your friend(s) together can make a difference?

Give yourself 10 points for every check!

Appendix
Cool Tools

This section offers the latest, most exciting, and best print materials plus Internet resources specifically designed to support strong and empowered girls like you:

Girls Guides and Teen Zines

Girls' Life Magazine
4517 Harford Road
Baltimore, MD 21214
www.girlslife.com

Seventeen Magazine
1440 Broadway
13th floor
New York, NY 10018
www.seventeen.com

YM
G+J USA Publishing
375 Lexington Avenue
New York, NY 10017-5514
www.ym.com

For Fun and Further Reading

*The Girl Pages: A Handbook of the Best Resources for Strong,
    Confident, Creative Girls*
(Girl Pages, 1st Ed) by Charlotte Milholland
Publisher: Hyperion, New York: 1999

*Brave New Girls: Creative Ideas to Help Girls Be Confident,
    Healthy, & Happy*
by Jeanette Gadeberg, Beth Hatlen (Illustrator)
Publisher: Fairview Press, Minneapolis: 1997

Girls Seen and Heard: 52 Life Lessons for Our Daughters
by The Ms. Foundation for Women, Sondra Forsyth, Carol Gilligan
    (Preface)
Publisher: Putnam Publishing Group, New York: 1998

GirlWise: How to Be Confident, Capable, Cool, and in Control
by Julia Devillers
Publisher: Prima Publishing, Roseville, California: 2002

*33 Things Every Girl Should Know: Stories, Songs, Poems and Smart
    Talk by 33 Extraordinary Women*
by Tonya Bolden (Editor)
Publisher: Crown Publishing Group, New York: 1998

*Hands On! 33 More Things Every Girl Should Know: Skills for Living
    Your Life from 33 Extraordinary Women-GLB*
by Suzanne Harper, Andrea Cascardi (Editor)
Publisher: Crown Publishing Group, New York: 2001

Picture the Girl: Young Women Speak Their Minds
by Audrey Shehyn
Publisher: Hyperion, New York: 2000

Girl Power: Young Women Speak Out
by Hillary Carlip
Publisher: Warner Books, New York: 1995

Girls to Women: Women to Girls
by Bunny McCune, Deb Traunstein
Publisher: Celestial Arts, Berkeley: 1998

For Girls Only: Wise Words, Good Advice
by Carol Weston
Publisher: William Morrow & Company, New York: 1998.

Internet resouces on following page

Super Sites

This list may seem short, but these sites have links to other sites—especially the link to Yahoo's list of e-zines.

~⊙ *www.freshangles.com*—A teen e-zine.

~⊙ *www.cyberteens.com*—A site with several areas of interest.

~⊙ *http://education.indiana.edu/cas/adol/adol.html*—Adolescence Directory Online, a service of Indiana University. Has many links to other sites.

~⊙ *http://dir.yahoo.com/Society_and_Culture/Cultures_and_Groups/Teenagers/Magazines/*—Yahoo.com's links to teen e-zines. This list has pretty much something for every interest.

~⊙ *www.gurl.com*—Gurl.com has many areas of interest for teenage girls.